THE RESOURCEFUL CHRISTIAN

The Resourceful Christian

A Guide to Surviving Lean Times

Kerry J. Koller

SERVANT BOOKS
Ann Arbor, Michigan

Published by Servant Books
P.O. Box 8617
Ann Arbor, Michigan 48107

Cover photo by John B. Leidy © Servant Publications
Book Design by John B. Leidy

Scripture quotations are from the *Revised Standard Version of the Bible*, copyrighted 1946, 1952 © 1971, 1973, and *The New American Bible*, copyright © 1970 by the Confraternity of Christian Doctrine, Washington, D.C., all rights reserved.

Printed in the United States of America
ISBN 0-89283-112-X

Contents

Preface

*Not that I complain of want; for I have learned, in whatever
state I am, to be content. I know how to be abased, and I know
how to abound; in any and all circumstances I have learned
the secret of facing plenty and hunger, abundance and want. I
can do all things in him who strengthens me.* (Phil 4:11-13)

Recently, a friend in Minneapolis did an economic study of that
city. He checked government statistics, went to the local
Multiple Listing Service, Chamber of Commerce, and any
other source of reliable information he could find. What he
discovered is startling.

The median annual family salary for the Minneapolis-St. Paul
area in 1979 was $18,800. A family of four, after paying personal
income taxes and social security payments, would have $13,800
a year, or $1,150 a month, left to spend. If they had purchased
the average home in their area and financed it through the
Federal Housing Administration, their monthly house payments would be around $690, including the mortgage, insur-
ance, and property taxes. On top of that would be another $142
a month to cover utilities and maintenance. If they owned a
medium-sized car and drove about 12,000 miles a year, they
could expect to pay about $235 a month for transportation. A
modest food budget would add another $235 to their monthly
payment schedule.

Housing, transportation, and food would cost this family
$1,291 a month. That is $141 more than their income!
Remember that this does not include medical expenses, clothing
costs, educational fees, personal items, life insurance premiums,
or money for recreation.

I double checked his figures against data available from the

U.S. Department of Labor, Bureau of Statistics. Their figures show that a middle-of-the-road budget for a four-member family in the Minneapolis-St. Paul area in 1979 was $21,426 annually. This is well above the median salary.

Most of us don't have to read reports like this or search government data sheets to know that something is not working right in the economy. The monthly exercise of paying the bills and balancing the checkbook brings the reality of the situation home in a clear and compelling way.

It was precisely this experience—trying to keep up with financial obligations and responsibilities in a world of increasing costs—which provided the occasion for this book. A number of Christians whom I associate with began to meet regularly to discuss the situation and to find some ways of coming to grips with what we experienced as an increasingly bleak and difficult economic situation.

Our discussion soon went beyond questions of how to save money by shopping sales, or what to look for when buying tools. We saw that there were deeper questions that needed to be answered before we could propose worthwhile solutions to our everyday problems. It is easy to assume that the economic future will be pretty much like the recent past, but that is far from certain. As we confronted that uncertainty we saw that we needed to look at how God wanted us to live in any case—in economic disaster or in economic boom. We soon found ourselves well beyond immediate temporal concerns and into questions of eternal life.

I decided to write this book because little that is written on this topic considers this fundamental "in any case" question. There are many suggestions about how to respond to a possible collapse of the economy, but little about what to do if things continue as they are or if they get better. The future is hidden from us, and although provident men and women prepare for the future, it is neither provident nor prudent to plan for only one kind of future.

I will set out some principles for shaping the economic and

financial aspects of your life. I will also apply these principles to the current economic situation and make some recommendations about specific courses of action to help you prepare for whatever the future holds. But my fundamental point is that the key to successfully negotiating the future involves not so much what you do as it does the kind of person you are. The goal is to become a provident and resourceful person, not just to do provident and resourceful things.

I write from an explicitly Christian point of view. However, this is not written solely for Christians, but for all men and women who are struggling to lead moral and responsible lives in the area of economics and finances. Principles drawn from scripture and the tradition and experience of 2,000 years of believers apply equally well to Christians and non-Christians because the principles are true. Anyone will benefit from having their life guided by true principles.

One difficulty in a book of this sort stems from the fact that our approach to money and material resources affects almost every aspect of our lives. However, my intention is not to address every aspect of life, but only one: to ask how we can marshall our economic and material resources in a way that can help us develop provident and resourceful character in the process? Hence, although I take our responsibility to help the poor and the disenfranchised as an essential part of Christian teaching, I do not deal with that question here. Nor do I deal with the entire area of depending upon God for our economic needs, as for example Mother Teresa and countless other heroic Christian men and women do every day. The failure to mention these things in the text is not an oversight, but simply a matter of sticking to the topic under discussion, that is, how can we learn to handle the resources we do have in a better way. For it is my belief that being responsible with our financial resources is essential to helping those in need. If we are not careful with what little we have, we won't have much to share with others. Further, those who live by faith, counting on God day by day for all their needs, must also be good stewards of what God gives them. Learning to be provident and resourceful does not excuse us from helping the needy or depending on God. It is a way of doing both better.

One other difficulty arises from the necessity of speaking to so many different kinds of people. I have tried to write so that the wealthy, the middle class, and the poor will all find help for developing their personal characters. But when it comes to speaking about specific economic situations, I put my sights on the average wage earner. Neither the poor nor the wealthy will find their economic experiences mirrored here.

Much of this book grew out of the study, research, and discussion of a particular group of people within a Christian community by the name of the People of Praise. Paul DeCelles directed the discussion, and Joe Bagiackas, Joel Kibler, Bud Rose, and Clem Walters consistently added key insights. Four persons who were part of that group made substantial contributions to the text of this work: Dan DeCelles, Patricia Lewsen, Ralph Whittenburg, and Jim Zwerneman. Tom Noe and Therese Cedergren oversaw the preparation of the manuscript. Although this book grew out of the work of that group, the final responsibility for its form and content rests entirely with the author.

ONE

Ease and Uncertainty

A GREEK PHILOSOPHER who lived 3,000 years ago first commented that the only thing that didn't change was the fact of change itself. Though he lived in a world totally unlike ours, he observed changes in nature and in his own feelings and experiences. If he could be transported into our century he would see that his maxim is still true, but he would stand amazed: change for us is more a fact of life than he could have ever predicted.

Imagine that he was able to revisit the earth once every century. He would probably be fairly comfortable with what he saw in every century up until around 1600. Not much would seem to have changed in the first twenty-six visits: travel by horse or by sail, people living in villages or small towns, with a few cities here and there, families staying in their hometowns for hundreds of years, people working in their homes. On his visit in 1700 he would probably sense something new happening, although it might not be very noticeable. In 1800 he would see the results of those stirrings which he sensed in 1700: industrialization on a large scale, families leaving their villages to work in a factory, travel by steam. The visit in 1900 would show even more changes: thorough mechanization of most industries, urbanization on a large scale. Even though he would have seen many changes in his last three visits, they would hardly prepare him for what he would see on his next visit, in the year 2000: electric lights, computers in homes, televisions, laser weapons, antibiotics, genetic engineering, trips to the moon, satellites in space, and other things that even we, living so close to the year 2000, can't predict. Yes, he was right about change. He could never have guessed how right he was.

Since man first appeared upon the earth until about 100 years ago, he lived without automobiles, refrigeration, radios, dishwashers, cameras, digital watches, and the like. These items, which we count necessary to our lives, were unknown 100 years ago. Many people alive today were born into a world in which none of these things existed. By the time they were adults, these things had become necessities of life.

The major changes which have shaped the modern world are not found in lists of inventions or scientific discoveries. The most significant changes are in attitudes and behavior. Many of these attitudinal and behavioral changes came about through the interplay of new inventions and everyday life. The automobile, for example, is the invention which has shaped much of life as we know it. It contributed to the decline of the pattern of neighborhood relationships, since those with cars were no longer dependent on those that lived around them for friendship—they could choose their friends, even ones across town. It also contributed to the demise of the neighborhood "mom and pop" stores, since one could travel to bigger stores with a larger selection and cheaper prices. Many other technical advances have similarly changed how we act and what we value. Many people are just now beginning to recognize the depth of these changes as they try to come to grips with handling money and material possessions.

Several key changes have had a massive effect upon us. They are relatively recent changes, which we are just now beginning to experience and which many of us need help adjusting to. The most fundamental has to do with the way we are taught to approach money and goods. Society used to encourage hard work, resourcefulness, thrift, and provident planning for the future. Today we are taught by society to get as much as we can and to put as little as possible into work. We are taught to put our trust in the economic system as a cornucopia of goods and services. We are taught to spend our money and to extend our liability through massive use of consumer credit. We are taught to be wasteful of natural resources. We are taught that specialists and repairmen will take care of our goods, and that for us to learn skills to care for and repair items is a waste of our precious time—time which could be spent "enjoying life" by watching television or buying more things to make us happy.

This change in mentality is quite recent—in fact, I can remember some things from my childhood which highlight this change. I came from a fairly large family, five boys and four girls. It was often difficult for my father to make enough money to support a family that large. We were never what you would call poor, but my father did work very hard, at times holding two full-time jobs just to make ends meet. I can remember watching my mother do the laundry on a scrub board, laboriously cranking the clothes through a hand wringer, hanging them out to dry on sunny days, and inside on rainy days. It was a big event when we got our first electric washer. No more wringing. No more scrub board. The saving in labor was tremendous. That washer became something of a symbol of a new way of life that we children were beginning to look forward to—a life free from drudgery, where machines would do many of the things which we found unenjoyable.

Many men today, faced with the difficult economic prospects which my father faced, would take another job only as a last resort. Their first choice would probably be to live on credit. Their second would be to send their wives to work and have the children cared for in day-care centers or by the schools. They would hesitate to sacrifice their free time—time for entertainment, recreation, and relaxation. Times have changed. Attitudes have changed. Values have changed.

Many of these changes are for the worse. They form our character in ways which leave us open to serious temptation in the area of money and possessions. Take, for example, the difference between operating on a cash basis and operating on credit.

Cash has a very definite reality to it. You can see it, feel it, count it. There is a fixed amount available in the world at any particular time. In transactions some of that money is transferred from one person to another in return for some identifiable good or service. When we deal with cash we are forced to ask realistic questions. How much do I have? How much can I spend? How much will this item cost? Should I spend my money on this or on something else? Should I save my money rather than spend it?

Credit, on the other hand, moves toward unreality and fantasy, because there is no clear limit to what we can buy. Credit is simply a promise to pay sometime after the goods or services have been acquired. It is a matter of good intentions, not hard facts: "Of course I intend to pay the money back—only a criminal would intend not to pay it back." It ushers in the fantasy that we can have things that we do not in fact have the money to purchase. This opens new and unrealistic possibilities for us and much of what we buy is based on mere desire for possessions.

Dealing in cash sets up an absolute limit beyond which one cannot go: you cannot purchase what you cannot pay for. We learn to keep our desires and fantasies in check. They are governed by the reality of how much we can actually spend. Credit removes these barriers and allows us to dream. This opens us to greed and other vices.

Greed is not only one of the results of consumer credit, it is also one of the causes of its widespread use and development. When you buy something on a bank card, not only do you have to pay the price of the good or service which you purchase, you also pay anywhere from 18-22% on the unpaid balance. The bank card was not invented out of humanitarian sentiment, but so that goods or services could generate greater profits for those who extend the credit. It serves the greed of the lender. But it is successful because the consumer is greedy too. He is unwilling to forego the purchase altogether, or even to wait until he can have the money to purchase it for its real value. He wants it so badly that he is willing to pay a premium of 20-50%.

Advertising is another cause of the attitudinal change. Advertising's role is to increase the rational freedom of the consumer by informing him of new products, of new features and refinements, of savings in cost, and so on. Unfortunately, certain trends in contemporary advertising have the net effect of enslaving rather than freeing the consumer. Much advertising is designed to keep our desires running high so that we find it difficult not to buy whatever the advertiser suggests.

It is easy to take advertising for granted and not think about it very much at all, unless we see something like a sexually suggestive ad. But even then we probably don't think about the system itself. In the long run the overall effect of the modern advertising system is more significant than the effect of any particular immoral advertisement. Advertising and other forces in our society can weaken the individual so that he becomes more open to suggestion, coercion, and manipulation. The future of modern society may indeed depend upon the ability of the individual to handle the power of modern means of communication.

Surely consumer credit and advertising have improved our standard of living and some of that has been good. But for Christians there is clear teaching about how to approach the things of this world. There are limits. The forces of consumer credit and manipulative advertising move those limits well beyond where God has said they should be. They encourage an unreality about money and persuade us to adopt the ideal of a comfortable and easy life.

The weakening of personal character is a direct threat to the survival of our free institutions of government. From the standpoint of a Christian, it is even more dangerous. An individual who is weakened by ideals of comfort and ease will soon be an easy target for the world, the flesh, and the devil. It is a matter of salvation to guard against being set upon by the powerful negative forces in our society.

A second major area of change in modern life is the weakening of the world economic system in general and the economy of the United States in particular. The fact that the supply of oil, which is essential to our way of life, has become unstable and expensive, has become something of a symbol of this problem.

Recently the Senate Committee on Energy reported that

America cannot become energy independent. The report stated that if we don't find some way to store significant amounts of oil, a Middle East crisis would cripple us. However, even if we continue to receive oil in an uninterrupted flow, the price will continue to rise in a way that will outstrip any increases in wages. Gasoline, oil for heating, plastics, synthetic fabrics, and other petroleum products will rise to a price which will force most of us to change our lives. If gasoline were $2.50 a gallon, many things in my life would change: I wouldn't drive to work as I do now; I wouldn't go across town to shows and restaurants; I'd do more in my own neighborhood; my wife would shop in the neighborhood although food might be cheaper somewhere else; my children wouldn't play sports across town; we'd stay closer to home for summer vacation. The list goes on—and this is just the impact of the cost of gasoline.

Not only is the price of oil high, but its supply will probably be interrupted. Such an interruption could devastate our economy. Walter Levy, one of the most respected experts on world oil, wrote recently:

> We will probably be confronted by a series of major oil crises which might take any or all of several forms: fighting for control over oil resources among importing countries or between the superpowers; an economic-financial crisis in importing countries; regional conflicts affecting the oil-producing area; or internal revolutions or upheavals in the Middle East. At best, it would appear that a series of future emergencies centering around oil will set back world progress for many, many years. And the world, as we know it now, will probably not be able to maintain its cohesion, nor be able to provide for the continued economic progress of its people against the onslaught of future oil shocks—with all that this might imply for the political stability of the West, its free institutions, and its internal and external security.[1]

Oil is not the only problem. Our system of food supply is quite efficient, supplying a large population with nutritious and tasty food at a relatively low cost. But the price of such efficiency is vulnerability. Our food system is highly specialized. For example, the Salinas Valley in California provides over 80% of all the lettuce produced in the U.S. Few regions produce everything needed for a healthy diet. Most of them concentrate on one or two major crops. The rest of what they need must be shipped to them. This means that our food supply is entirely dependent upon the transportation industry. A truckers' strike, higher costs of fuel, etc., would have very definite effects on the availability of food. Even if food is available its cost will continue to rise, not only because of inflation but also because fuels continue to rise in price. Many of us will have to change our diet—we will simply be unable to pay for the kind of food we now eat.

We are highly vulnerable when it comes to the necessities of life. The problems, however, are deeper than the uncertainty of uninterrupted supplies of food and energy. The entire world economic system is in a disarray that probably will not be straightened out within the next decade. The world monetary system presently has no commodity which supports money and its value. In fact, money, which in the past has always been a means for acquiring commodities, has itself become a commodity. That is why people now talk about the "money market." Money itself is bought and sold. This lack of foundation introduces tremendous instability into the entire system.

Further, the mechanisms of banking and exchange of money need to be completely overhauled if they are to support the increased level of world trade and finance necessary for future economic growth. The current framework is hopelessly outdated. Rampant inflation, energy-caused trade-balance deficits, and declining productivity have caused it severe damage. We will not see global economic stability until the monetary system is restructured.

We are faced with a very dangerous situation. The ideals which the economic system promotes are increasingly materialistic. We are told that our happiness lies in comfort and ease, and that the acquisition of goods and services is the key to that happiness. This makes us increasingly dependent upon money and all that it can buy. Ironically, the economic system itself is less and less able to deliver what it promises. Indeed, it is increasingly unable to guarantee us what are normally called "necessities of life." At the same time that we are told about the joys of owning a home video system with a six-foot screen, we observe that it is increasingly difficult for us to buy food or to operate our cars. It is ironic that, just as materialistic values are being loudly proclaimed, we find the economic system unable to supply the very things which the materialist has promised. This is dangerous, but it is also a great help, since the more obvious it becomes that we cannot depend upon the economic system for the happiness we seek, the less chance there is that we will be ensnared by it.

But even though we may resist the temptation to define life in materialistic terms, we are still affected by the current approach to money and finances. It has already affected our character and our attitudes. In preaching happiness as ease and comfort, and in promising us that the economic machinery of the world would produce that happiness, it has taught us to be less thrifty, less self-reliant, less responsible.

These two major changes in American economic life—ease as the ideal, and economic uncertainty as the reality—pose a significant challenge. How are we to respond to the massive influence of consumer credit, advertising, and the comfort-oriented lifestyle they breed? What is the right approach to economic responsibility in a time of serious economic uncertainty?

TWO

New Men and New Women

A MERICAN LIFE HAS UNDERGONE profound changes in recent times. Our response to these changes must be to become new men and new women. Such change in us is the key to the only adequate response to the negative effect which the new economic situation has had upon our lives. We need to recapture a provident and resourceful way of life. We must change many of our attitudes, many of the values which the world economic system has trained us to accept, and many of the ways in which we presently handle our money and our property. This change will mean going back to a way of life similar in some respects to that of our parents and grandparents. It will mean moving away from consumerism, credit, and manipulation by advertising. It will mean moving towards thriftiness, prudent planning for the future, the wise use of resources, and a totally scriptural framework for managing money and possessions.

But this change must be more than external. We need to become provident and resourceful *persons*. This is more important than simply doing provident and resourceful things. Although the doing is important to the development of the character traits, it is not the same thing. Being provident has to do with how we view the future and how we use today's resources in the light of the future.

A friend of mine lived in a city where the top civil service positions were filled by patronage. If you belonged to the same political party as the mayor and had worked for his election, you could count on an increase in pay and a promotion. Of course, if your party lost the next election you could be demoted with a resulting loss in pay. My friend's friend, with the election of the new mayor, found himself promoted to a position which paid considerably more than he had received in the past. The question was how to live with this higher income. Instead of choosing to elevate his life-style to match his higher income, he decided to live as he had always lived, and bank the difference between the old and new paycheck. He knew that it would be difficult in the future to step down in style of life, so he chose a simpler, more stable way of living while building up cash reserves. If his pay was cut back in the future he would survive it easily.

The provident person usually has an emergency supply of the necessities of life, not only money but other necessities. Most Americans buy food from week to week, just enough to last until the next time they shop, with no food reserve. If a truckers' strike or a storm hit their area, they would be in sorry shape. Storing up food, money, extra clothing, fuel, replacement parts for essential tools, etc., is one mark of a provident person.

The provident person also has some goals in mind and works patiently and consistently toward the attainment of those goals. He is not discouraged because it takes work and time, but he works at it until he achieves what he wants. The woman who makes it a goal to can a certain amount of each kind of vegetable and works all through the autumn to do it is a good example of a provident person. She has plenty of other things to do, but she works at accomplishing her goals.

Being resourceful, on the other hand, has to do with using resources in an appropriate way. One of the most important resources of a resourceful person is himself. He learns how to do things, acquires the kinds of skills that a person needs in order to use, form, make, and repair the many things he uses in his life. A resourceful man has tools, takes care of them, knows how to use them and, in fact, does use them. If a resourceful woman has a sewing machine, she takes care of it and uses it well. A resourceful man or woman is a "jack of all trades, and a master of some."

A resourceful person seeks quality items, rather than the faddish, the shoddy, the cheap. A resourceful person also repairs things rather than simply discarding them. In the interest of ease and comfort, many people would prefer to call the repairman or go out and buy a replacement, rather than repair things themselves. A resourceful person is able to maintain his home and equipment and is not totally dependent on the serviceman.

Recently, I received an interesting letter from a friend, which illustrates the problem:

Last summer I was fortunate enough to take a vacation with my family in and around Smokey Mountain National Park. We had a couple of interesting experiences, one of which was going to a spot called Cade's Cove. It is a long valley in the middle of the mountains. From 100 to 150 years ago it was inhabited by as many as 650 people, living in very rustic, even primitive, circumstances. The buildings are fairly well preserved. We really got a sense for how these people lived. We visited rude one-room cabins, each built over a root cellar, with a very small loft. Almost everything inside is made out of wood—hand-carved door latches, windows, and furniture. The living space is very small. Many of the cabins are two or three miles apart. We saw primitive barns, mills for grinding grain, and the remains of a blacksmith's shop. Cade's Cove gave me a sense of how people used to live, relying on their own skills, their ability to work with their hands, to work the earth, to survive without much outside help.

Where I grew up, people could not directly provide themselves with very much at all. In the Bronx, in an apartment complex called Parkchester—12,500 apartments owned by the Metropolitan Life Insurance Company—we did not fix anything that broke. As a matter of fact, the landlord did not want us to. He wanted the fuses and faucet washers replaced by the building maintenance man. I grew up in the kind of society where everyone depended immediately on the serviceman, the specialist, the supplier, to take care of even the smallest needs. I knew, as most of us in our school knew, that all those good things we were able to get to eat did in fact grow in the frozen food department of the local grocery store. I and the children I grew up with expected to move upward economically. And we were trained that security depended not so much on acquiring skills as on acquiring money. A whole educational spiral was set in motion for me and for the kids I grew up with, oriented toward larger and larger income-producing jobs.

We are far less provident and resourceful than our ancestors. Extreme specialization has deprived many of us of the skills necessary to produce and maintain the services and commodities needed for our daily lives.

Often we are not educated in provident and resourceful attitudes and skills because we do not think that they are very important. But they are essential to our everyday life.

The world is changing around us, and we must change to meet the challenge. Deciding not to change is itself a decision to be formed by worldly attitudes and to place oneself at the mercy of the world economic system.

We need to take specific steps to protect ourselves in case the economic situation gets worse. More importantly, we need to effect a character change within ourselves. It is not simply a matter of changing some of our behavior; it is a matter of changing our character.

Most of us learn as we get older that some foods, which we used to be able to devour with impunity, now put pounds on us. I have learned the hard way that going on diets only brings temporary relief. If I return to my regular eating habits, the pounds go right back on. The only way to straighten things out is to change the *way* I eat and my *attitude* toward food. Today we have the same kind of situation in the sphere of economics. We might take this or that action, but unless we change our consumerist mentality, training ourselves to resist the efforts of those forces in our society promoting a worldly mindset, we will not be able to cope successfully.

One of the first steps in making the changes I am suggesting is to take stock of your present situation. Examine your current attitudes and life-style. How are you handling your money now? Do you have a budget, or do you just spend your money on what you want at the moment you want it?

Having a budget is essential to making headway. A budget gives you control of how you spend your money, provides a record of the past, and is an important device for assessing your current economic situation. Later I will give a fuller treatment of how to budget, but at this point it is important to see how you are managing your money. A budget should list all those things which you are obliged to pay: regular support for the Lord's work, house payments or rent, food, utilities, clothing, medical expenses, transportation, etc. It is not simply a record of how you spent your money, but an aid in controlling expenses. In each of these categories you should write down how much you will spend and stick to it. The tough, but absolutely essential part is not to spend more in any category than you have written down. This takes discipline and self-control, but it is the only way to get mastery over your finances.

When you first use a budget you might discover that the amount of money spent in any category is considerably more than you allocated. This means that either the original amount was inaccurate, or that you are spending more than you should. You have to make an honest reassessment of the situation. If you need more money in a category, assign it. Of course, assigning more money to one category means that it has to be taken from another. This leads to further reassessments and decisions. Do you need this more than that? Do you make enough money at your present job? Should you change jobs or take an extra job?

This kind of exercise is important not simply because it puts order in your spending, but because it forces you to take responsible action. When you have to ask about money for this rather than that, you are moving toward a more realistic life-style. Confronting choices and making decisions forms valuable character traits.

Many times people make budgets with all the right intentions but do not stick to them. Often they simply forget about them and return to their earlier way of doing things. Sometimes they stick to them in some categories but then spend their remaining funds in wildly extravagant ways. A person who does not have enough money to pay his bills might buy something frivolous— an expensive camera, another pair of shoes, or an unneeded suit. This is a temptation to be resisted. It is a matter of discipline and strength. If you feel that you do not have the strength, find a friend or clergyman to encourage and aid you. After you successfully resist the temptation a few times you will gain enough strength to resist it more effectively in the future.

Another area to consider has to do with your desire for material goods. Have you been deeply influenced by advertising and the media? Have you internalized a strong desire to possess things, to have money, to live "comfortably?" These are all to be resisted. One of the best ways to do this is to put yourself out of the reach of most advertising. If television affects you, cut back on your viewing. If it is the newspaper, stop reading the ads except when you have to. Attitudes have a cause. If you remove the cause, you will go a long way toward removing the attitude. Often, however, this is not enough because the problem is within us. We have to repent of the desires we have, admitting that they are wrong, seeking God's forgiveness, and deciding that we will act differently in the future.

A key to meeting the challenges of our time is the recovery of a provident and resourceful style of life. But we do not want simply to recover a specific way of life—we want to recover a Christian way of life. Before we proceed to discuss the details of how to live providently and resourcefully, we need to have a totally Christian framework for managing money and possessions.

.

THREE

A Scriptural Perspective

BEING PROVIDENT AND RESOURCEFUL is one thing; being a provident and resourceful Christian is another. The provident and resourceful Christian allows his entire attitude to be formed by God's word through scripture and church teaching. Five principles, drawn from scripture, form the foundation of a Christian mentality about money and finances. These principles are essential to Christians forming their response to the challenges of today's world.

1. The form of this world is passing away.

2. The economic systems of this world are one of God's ways to provide for his creatures.

3. God's provision has a twofold purpose, to give us enough resources to support his work and to provide for our sustenance. He calls us to put his work first.

4. We should always live in a way that prepares us for economic change.

5. As we prepare for the future, we want to take seriously the scriptural warnings about the dangers that accompany the pursuit or possession of wealth.

In this chapter we will focus on the first of these principles.

The first thing to realize is that there are real dangers in focusing on financial matters. We can become so concerned about material things and earthly goods that we lose sight of the goal. We need to have God's perspective in order to avoid developing a wrong perspective. For this we look to scripture. In his first letter to the Corinthians, Paul tells us that "the form of this world is passing away" (1 Cor 7:31).

When we deal with money, possessions, economics, and the like, it is important to develop a perspective that is not limited to the usual framework of human time. The psalmist sees time as God wants us to see it.

Lord, thou hast been our dwelling place
   in all generations.
Before the mountains were brought forth,
   or ever thou hadst formed the earth and the world,
   from everlasting to everlasting thou art God.

Thou turnest man back to the dust,
   and sayest, "Turn back, O children of men!"
For a thousand years in thy sight
   are but as yesterday when it is past,
   or as a watch in the night.

Thou dost sweep men away; they are like a dream,
   like grass which is renewed in the morning:
in the morning it flourishes and is renewed;
   in the evening it fades and withers.

For we are consumed by thy anger;
   by thy wrath we are overwhelmed.
Thou hast set our iniquities before thee,
   our secret sins in the light of thy countenance.

For all our days pass away under thy wrath,
   our years come to an end like a sigh.
The years of our life are threescore and ten,
   or even by reason of strength fourscore;
yet their span is but toil and trouble;
     they are soon gone, and we fly away.

> Who considers the power of thy anger,
>> and thy wrath according to the fear of thee?
> So teach us to number our days
>> that we may get a heart of wisdom.
>> (Ps 90:1-12)

Our perception of time changes as we progress from infancy through adolescence, into maturity and old age. Children think in terms of what is most immediate to them—the needs and events of the day, even of the minute. Tell a young child that Christmas is six months away, and he will not be able to understand the length of time involved. The next day he might ask, "Is it Christmas *now?*" Later in life, perhaps as a teenager, he will be able to think in terms of longer spans of time. "Next summer I will try to get a job in the factory." "When I graduate from high school I want to go to college." In fact, one of the signs of adulthood and maturity is the ability to think in terms of the span of one's life. At each stage of life, our awareness of time broadens. We begin to regulate our immediate needs and desires in relation to our long-term needs and desires.

I recall my father telling me, "It may seem like the days drag now, but wait until you're my age and you'll see that things go by very quickly." As our perspective on time changes, our perspective on life changes also. As a young man, a friend of mine once attended the funeral of a man in his sixties. Most of those who attended the services were elderly people. They talked about their lives in ten- and twenty-year segments. My friend, in his mid-twenties at the time, felt odd as they talked about segments of their lives which were equal in span to his *entire* life. Their viewpoints were broader and larger than his; they had experienced more of life and their perspectives differed in many ways from his.

As we grow in age and maturity, our perspective on life changes from short-term to long-term. We begin to think differently about what we find valuable and what we find worthless. We begin to see things in light of the entire process of our lives. We realize that we won't live forever. Often, it is this realization of our impending death that first prompts us to take that careful, slow, long-term look at life. We read in the Psalms, "The years of our life are threescore and ten, or even by reason of strength fourscore; yet their span is but toil and trouble; they are soon gone, and we fly away" (Ps 90:10).

It is natural to see our lives like dust blown across the silent desert, to see death as the impassable barrier. But we also read, "So teach us to number our days that we may get a heart of wisdom" (Ps 90:12). Only the man with a heart of wisdom can see beyond a view of death that takes no assessment of eternity. For him, life extends into eternity, and his decisions are made in terms of this larger perspective.

Yet, in a certain sense, even the level of spiritual wisdom which allows us to see beyond our own death is incomplete. This coming of Christ has given new urgency to this ancient mystery of the passing of time. It is no longer sufficient simply to act with wisdom in view of our personal death. Rather, we must act wisely in light of an even larger perspective, one that takes into account the end of time itself. Our individual death—the end of time for each of us—is assumed under a larger happening, a part of God's plan that is rapidly coming to fulfillment: "The appointed time has grown very short. . . . For the form of this world is passing away" (1 Cor 7:29, 31). History will come to a close at a certain point, and the spiritual man must guide his decisions so that he takes into account not only his personal death, but also the death of the universe, the climax and culmination of God's creative action.

Carl Sagan, the astronomer, developed an interesting calendar in which all history is compressed into one year. He made January 1 the time in prehistory that some scientists call the "big bang," when all the created matter might have exploded outward from the center of the universe. January 1 of the following year is the present. Sagan then fits the major events for which scientists have evidence into this year's span. The day on which our galaxy coalesces is around May 1. The planet earth solidifies around September. It is not until the first day of

December that an atmosphere with a significant amount of oxygen begins to form. Halfway through that month our fellow creatures begin to appear. On Christmas Eve the first dinosaurs appear. On New Year's Eve, around 10:30 p.m., Adam and Eve walk the face of the earth. Four minutes before midnight, the most recent period of glaciation begins. One second before midnight, Columbus discovers America. All recorded history occupies only the final ten seconds of the calendar year.

This image helps us to understand that God is "from everlasting to everlasting." The life of an individual, compared with the life of the universe, is like a snap of the fingers. Like a wildflower, which withers when it is cut, the life of a human being is a small thing on the scale of the whole of creation. The Lord existed before creation; he will exist after creation comes to its climax. It is simply a matter of realism for us to consider the fragility of our life on earth. Here, but for a moment, the major part of our existence will occur after our individual death, when we come into eternity.

The New Testament often suggests that our personal realization of the nearness of death and the debt which each of us must pay to death is an opportunity to form a new perspective on life. When we first confront the fact that we must die, it changes us. As God reveals to us personally—either through scripture or through experiential contact with death—that there is a final end to all things, his purpose is to influence our behavior. "The form of this world is passing away" looks like a simple statement of fact. In reality it is a principle which God expects us to use to moderate our style of life.

And he said to them, "Take heed, and beware of all covetousness; for a man's life does not consist in the abundance of his possessions." And he told them a parable, saying, "The land of a rich man brought forth plentifully; and he thought to himself, 'What shall I do, for I have nowhere to store my crops?' And he said, 'I will do this: I will pull down my barns, and build larger ones; and there I will store all my grain and my goods. And I will say to my soul, Soul, you have ample goods laid up for many years; take your ease, eat, drink, be merry.' But God said to him, 'Fool! This night your soul is required of you; and the things you have prepared, whose will they be?' So is he who lays up treasure for himself, and is not rich toward God."

(Lk 12:15-21)

Our death is not a distant experience which has no bearing on daily behavior.

The wise man realizes that he is going to die and lives his life accordingly. He is especially careful regarding the proper use of this world's treasures with regard to the needs of his fellow men.

There was a rich man, who was clothed in purple and fine linen and who feasted sumptuously every day. And at his gate lay a poor man named Lazarus, full of sores, who desired to be fed with what fell from the rich man's table; moreover the dogs came and licked his sores. The poor man died and was carried by the angels to Abraham's bosom. The rich man also died and was buried; and in Hades, being in torment, he lifted up his eyes, and saw Abraham far off and Lazarus in his bosom. And he called out, "Father Abraham, have mercy upon me, and send Lazarus to dip the end of his finger in water and cool my tongue; for I am in anguish in this flame." But Abraham said, "Son, remember that you in your lifetime received your good things, and Lazarus in like manner evil things; but now he is comforted here, and you are in anguish. And besides all this, between us and you a great chasm has been fixed, in order that those who would pass from here to you may not be able, and none may cross from there to us."

(Lk 16:19-26)

The use of the goods of this world is regulated by the justice of God. Those who have kept for themselves an excess of this world's goods will be punished in the life to come. On the other side of death, God's standard will be invoked. Sitting in judgment, he will redress the inequities and injustices of this world.

The rich man and the poor man alike will find that whatever possessions they have acquired, whatever they own, will fail them on the night their souls are required of them. That time will come for every one of us, and no amount of possessions will gain us access to the bosom of Abraham. It may get us into a prestigious country club, but it won't get us into the only club that counts, where a lifetime membership means eternity. Indeed, for many, the pursuit of earthly treasures is an obstacle, preventing them from finding eternal treasure.

There is wisdom to be acquired from meditating on and understanding what it means that we are here only for a short time. One thing we can learn is to distinguish the means from the end. All of us have only one end ultimately, the end for which we were made. We may choose our own goals of various sorts, but we were made by someone else. We are his. We belong to him and he has an end for each of us—to live with him forever. This is our end, toward which all our efforts must be directed.

God has put other created things in our care, and we have to view these as means for attaining our end. The fellow who thought, I've got enough laid up for myself in my barns, so I'm going to eat, drink, and be merry, had a very short-term perspective. He could not see much farther than a few years ahead. A short-term perspective leads to an approach to life in which we focus on things—acquiring, enjoying, and thinking of ways to protect our possessions. Our decisions will all be geared toward how they will enhance our material well-being and our pleasure.

A long-term perspective, however, tells us that we will be judged not by what we have possessed, but by how we have used our possessions. Did we use them as a means for attaining our end? Two scripture passages are especially helpful in seeing this.

> He said also to the man who had invited him, "When you give a dinner or a banquet, do not invite your friends or your brothers or rich neighbors, lest they also invite you in return, and you be repaid. But when you give a feast, invite the poor,

the maimed, the lame, the blind, and you will be blessed, because they cannot repay you. You will be repaid at the resurrection of the just." (Lk 14:12-13)

As for the rich in this world, charge them not to be haughty, nor to set their hopes on uncertain riches but on God who richly furnishes us with everything to enjoy. They are to do good, to be rich in good deeds, liberal and generous, thus laying up for themselves a good foundation for the future, so that they may take hold of the life which is life indeed. (1 Tm 6:17-19)

Don't think of repayment within a short period of time, like a year or two years, or even fifty years. Instead, use your material possessions according to God's plan, and be repaid on the long term, at the resurrection of the just. Receive now a treasure in heaven that does not fail.

FOUR

God Provides for
All His Creatures

THE SECOND PRINCIPLE is that the economic system of the world is one of the ways in which God makes provision for all his creatures. Psalm 104 shows the Lord provides for all of us—the worms, the dinosaurs, and mankind—in marvelous and complex ways.

> Thou makest springs gush forth in the valleys;
>   they flow between the hills,
> they give drink to every beast of the field;
>   the wild asses quench their thirst.
> By them the birds of the air have their habitation;
>   they sing among the branches.
> From thy lofty abode thou waterest the mountains;
>   the earth is satisfied with the fruit of thy work.
> Thou dost cause grass to grow for the cattle,
>   and plants for man to cultivate,
> that he might bring forth food from the earth,
>   and wine to gladden the heart of man." (Ps 104:10-15)

God takes care of all his creatures, not just his own people. "Love your enemies and pray for those who persecute you, so that you may be sons of your Father who is in heaven; for he makes his sun rise on the evil and on the good, and sends rain on the just and on the unjust" (Mt 5:44-45). The evil have farms, and God sends his sun and rain to nourish their crops just as he does to the crops of the just.

If we look at how God has distributed the resources of this earth, the various climatological conditions, and the talents of men, we see that his creation suggests a system of cooperation and trade meant to be beneficial to all. One part of the world is rich in iron ore, another in coal. Through trade, both can make steel. You can send wheat from the United States to another part of the world and come back with tin, coffee, and oil. Mutual cooperation among the peoples of the earth should result in a way of distributing natural resources according to God's plan.

This cooperative effort which economic interdependence brings about is also important because it furthers God's goal of developing brotherhood in the entire human race. Cooperation brings people together in towns, villages, and cities, where they begin to share their lives. It forms the basis of human culture and the great tapestry of human history. In this world order God works out all that he has in mind for mankind.

This affects Christians in two ways. First, we are involved in the world economy because it is the way God provides for our needs. Our participation can help in the provision for all, because of our sensitivity to God's plan. God entrusts the administration of this overall distribution plan largely to human authorities, and he holds them accountable for meeting the material needs of people. The inequitable distribution of material resources is due to sin in the world, to greed and the abuse of authority. God set the world up to work right: there is enough of everything for everyone to be taken care of.

Second, we are primarily obliged to be good citizens diligently engaged in productive work, helping the whole system to operate properly. We should also participate in the political life of our community in order to promote the good of all by influencing society toward God's purposes. We also further God's plan by ministering to the poor and by giving alms.

These are good reasons to stay involved in the world around us and its economic system, but we should not be naive about our involvement in the world. Although Jesus has overcome sin, the world is still vulnerable to the power of the evil one. When we become involved in the world we run real risks of being cheated, of being corrupted, of being persecuted.

There are, as we all know, wicked persons, rich and powerful, who will take advantage of good men and women for their own sinful gain. "Is it not the rich men among you who haul you into court? Is it not the rich who blaspheme the name of Jesus?" (Jas 2:6-7). Getting cheated out of our money would not be so terrible, except that it is actually God's money, given to us to be used for his purposes. The real crime is that God's money is stolen, diverted from his purposes, and used for sinful purposes. We cannot lay all the blame at the feet of the rich, of course. We know that "all have sinned and fallen short of the glory of God" (Rom 3:23). Just as there are wicked men who are rich and powerful, there are wicked men who are poor, not necessarily because of the wickedness of the rich, but because of their own wickedness: laziness, irresponsibility, self-indulgence, immorality. The wicked who are poor have their own schemes for diverting God's money from his purposes into their pockets.

Jesus tells us that we run another risk by being part of the world. "If you were of the world, the world would love its own; but because you are not of the world, but I chose you out of the world, therefore the world hates you" (Jn 15:19). Some men and women will persecute us simply because we're Christians. If economic conditions worsen, persecution can be expected to increase. Are Christians going to be able to turn for help to those who hate and persecute them now? It's not likely. Will economic difficulties improve our chances of keeping legitimate tax exemptions? Probably not. Will church-affiliated schools be looked upon more kindly? Probably less kindly. In difficult times our hope is not in the world but in the name of the Lord and in one another.

Even with all the risks, God, who loves us very much, tells us to remain involved in the world and its structures.

I do not pray that thou shouldst take them out of the world, but that thou shouldst keep them from the evil one. They are not of the world, even as I am not of the world. Sanctify them in the truth; thy word is truth. As thou didst send me into the world, so I have sent them into the world. (Jn 17:15-18)

Be subject for the Lord's sake to every human institution, whether it be to the emperor as supreme, or to governors as sent by him to punish those who do wrong and to praise those who do right. For it is God's will that by doing right you should put to silence the ignorance of foolish men. Live as free men, yet without using your freedom as a pretext for evil; but live as servants of God. Honor all men. Love the brotherhood. Fear God. Honor the emperor. (1 Pt 2:13-17)

Another reason for Christians' involvement in the world is a strategic one. We want to bring the good news of salvation to all people, to deliver them from the kingdom of darkness, and to bring them into the kingdom of light, to build the kingdom of Christ on earth. "You are the light of the world. A city set on a hill cannot be hid. Nor do men light a lamp and put it under a bushel, but on a stand, and it gives light to all in the house. Let your light so shine before men, that they may see your good works and give glory to your Father who is in heaven" (Mt 5:14-16). We must be involved with people if we are to reach them. They must be able, at least, to see our good works.

Because of the complex nature of the twentieth century, to be involved in the world means to rely heavily on its systems. We are in the thick of it, up to our eyebrows, and that is the position that God wants us to be in. However, we need to protect ourselves from being at a disadvantage if times worsen. Being provident in the face of this means working toward a position that will prudently combine economic independence, opportunities for effective evangelism, and opportunities for cooperating with God's overall plan for providing for mankind's needs.

FIVE

God's Work Comes First

THE THIRD PRINCIPLE is that God's provision has a twofold purpose: first, to give us enough resources to enable us to support his work and, second, to provide for our sustenance. He calls us to put his work first.

> The point is this: he who sows sparingly will also reap sparingly, and he who sows bountifully will also reap bountifully. Each one must do as he has made up his mind, not reluctantly or under compulsion, for God loves a cheerful giver. And God is able to provide you with every blessing in abundance, so that you may always have enough of everything and may provide in abundance for every good work. As it is written, "He scatters abroad, he gives to the poor; his righteousness endures for ever." He who supplies seed to the sower and bread for food will supply and multiply your resources and increase the harvest of your righteousness. You will be enriched in every way for great generosity, which through us will produce thanksgiving to God. (2 Cor 9:6-11)

Paul is telling us that God provides us with money to live on and money to give away; we don't have to choose between the two. The Revised Standard Version's rendering of the final verse implies that God will enrich us *in return* for our generosity. A better way to understand the passage is to say that God will enrich us *to enable* us to give more generously. As God looks over the whole earth and what he wants to accomplish, he looks for men and women who will use money for his purposes. When he finds them he gives money to them.

Another implication of this principle is that in every paycheck, regardless of how small it may seem, there are two parts: one for our sustenance, the other for good works. Good works do not come out of our excess. What is left over after we provide for God's work will be sufficient for our needs. If you've used your whole paycheck for yourself, God could legitimately take back the part that you should have used for him.

Recognizing the two purposes in God's provision, we also see a difference in their priorities. "But seek first his kingdom and his righteousness, and all these things shall be yours as well" (Mt 6:33). We want first of all to put our funds into building God's dwelling place among men, and second into insulation for our own houses (see Hg 1:2-4).

But what happens when times get harder and it's more difficult to support God's work? "I charge you in the presence of God and of Christ Jesus who is to judge the living and the dead, and by his appearing and his kingdom: preach the word, be urgent in season and out of season" (2 Tm 4:1-2). When you think you can afford it and when you think you can't, when times are good and when times are bad—no matter what—be engaged in preaching the word and supporting the apostolic work. We need to be engaged in God's work, regardless of the state of the economy. In fact, while we can afford it and while times are good, we want to set aside some of our resources for the days when it will be more difficult to fund God's work (1 Cor 16:1-3).

Should hard times come upon us, we are commanded to be ready to sacrifice our material well-being rather than to abandon God's work. Consider the Christians in Macedonia, whom Paul holds up as an example of generous giving.

> We want you to know, brethren, about the grace of God which has been shown in the churches of Macedonia, for in a severe test of affliction, their abundance of joy and their

extreme poverty have overflowed in a wealth of liberality on their part. For they gave according to their means, as I can testify, and beyond their means, of their own free will, begging us earnestly for the favor of taking part in the relief of the saints. (2 Cor 8:1-4)

All they had in abundance was joy. But they gave according to their means and even beyond their means, even begging for the favor of giving. That is the kind of people we want to be, giving past the point of hurting, for the sake of God's work.

God assures us that, as we spend money now for his purposes, we will be repaid in the days to come. We can gladly endure suffering, hardship, and privation in these days, knowing God's promise.

What are the good works that scripture calls us to support financially? First, we are to support the work of the elders, especially those who rule well and those who work in preaching and teaching (see 1 Tm 5:17-18), along with those who do missionary work (see Phil 4:14-18). We should be giving regularly to our church, fellowship, or Christian community. The pastors of our churches and communities need to be supported so that they can continue the work God has given them. The church and its work, its mission and apostolate, need to be supported.

We are also enjoined to show hospitality to strangers and to support widows, orphans, and those who are poor through no fault of their own (see 1 Tm 5:3-9; Rom 15:26). Almsgiving is something that Jesus urges upon us; it has always been a part of the life of the Christian people. An elder in the early church encouraged his people to almsgiving and works of mercy with these words:

Almsgiving embraces under the single name of mercy many excellent works of devotion, so that the good intentions of all the faithful may be of equal value, even where their means are not. The love that we owe both God and man is always free from any obstacle that would prevent us from having a good intention. The angels sang: "Glory to God in the highest, and peace to his people on earth." The person who shows love and compassion to those in any kind of affliction is blessed, not only with the virtue of good will but also with the gift of peace.

The works of mercy are innumerable. Their very variety brings this advantage to those who are true Christians, that in the matter of almsgiving not only the rich and affluent but also those of average means and the poor are able to play their part. Those who are unequal in their capacity to give can be equal in the love within their hearts.[2]

Almsgiving is not simply "do-goodism." It is part of the work of God, and it is spiritual. A man I know who spent some time in India said that everywhere he went things were very bad. Not only was there great poverty, sickness, and suffering, but there seemed to be a great spiritual depression across the land. It affected him so much that, although he was in a country which he would probably never be able to visit again, he simply could not bring himself to take pictures. He did not want to remember any of it. He was able, though, to visit the place where Mother Teresa and her associates were ministering to the poor and sick. He found that there people were smiling. He was confronting a new spiritual reality. God was ministering to the poor through his people, bringing his own Spirit into the situation.

Prepared for Change

T HE FOURTH PRINCIPLE is that we should always live in a way that prepares us for economic change. Scripture and the experience of mankind unite to tell us that economic conditions do change. "In the time of plenty think of the time of hunger; in the days of wealth think of poverty and need. From morning to evening conditions change, and all things move swiftly before the Lord" (Sir 18:25-26). Throughout history, circumstances of varying degrees of gravity have brought about significant economic changes for the worse. Seasonal changes, inflationary trends, shifts in trade patterns, depression, famine, plague, war—things quickly go from good to bad. Most of us grew up expecting things to change, certainly, but only for the good! The gross national product is supposed to increase; salaries are supposed to go up; the consumer price index is supposed to go down. Our approach to the future is often unrealistic, and, consequently, irresponsible.

Currently we live in a time of plenty, which by many economic indexes surpasses any age preceding it. But scripture warns us that it is in just such times as these that we should recall times of hunger, times of poverty, times of need. Moreover, there are signs everywhere that the times could grow increasingly worse from an economic point of view. Just how much worse and for how long we do not know. But scripture tells us that we should take precautionary measures. "A prudent man sees danger and hides himself; but the simple go on, and suffer for it" (Prv 22:3).

To live providently means to set aside a portion of today's plenty for tomorrow's need. To live resourcefully means to develop the skills and capabilities for producing and maintaining a larger proportion of the goods that are essential to our lives. "In the morning sow your seed, and at evening withhold not your hand [do your farmwork during the morning, but when you come home produce something else, engage in another trade]; for you do not know which will prosper" (Eccl 11:6). As we look toward the future, we are to be flexible, resourceful, able to do more than one thing to take care of our needs. Proverbs 31:13-25 provides us with the example of a provident and resourceful woman. She is flexible and knows a variety of skills to meet changing times. If we approach our economic future providently and resourcefully, we, like the woman in Proverbs 31, will be "clothed in strength and dignity." We, too, will be in a position to "laugh at the time to come."

Right about now you might find yourself becoming a little uneasy with this approach. What about living by faith? Doesn't scripture forbid the laying up of treasures? Isn't this actually relying more on man's efforts than on God's?

These are all good questions. Many well-intentioned, devout, and intelligent Christians have looked at the same texts and come up with different answers to them. These are also difficult questions. However, my interpretation is not a new one. That a person has a responsibility to care for himself, that he can possess material goods, and can own more than he needs at the present moment, has been held by the majority of Christian teachers throughout the centuries (for example, Thomas Aquinas, Luther, Calvin, the social encyclicals of the Catholic Church, etc.). At the same time, this teaching acknowledges our complete dependence upon God and points out the dangers inherent in the possession and use of material goods.

This brings us to the fifth principle: As we prepare for the future, we must heed scripture's warnings about the temptations that can beseige the man intent on pursuing and possessing wealth. These temptations include temptations to excessive solicitude (anxiety) for temporal goods, covetousness, idolatry, dishonesty, and showing partiality to the rich. I will consider them in that order.

The first is anxiety.

Therefore I tell you, do not be anxious about your life, what you shall eat or what you shall drink, nor about your body, what you shall put on. Is not life more than food, and the body more than clothing? Look at the birds of the air: they neither sow nor reap nor gather into barns, and yet your heavenly Father feeds them. Are you not of more value than they? And which of you by being anxious can add one cubit to his span of life? And why are you anxious about clothing? Consider the lilies of the field, how they grow; they neither toil nor spin; yet I tell you, even Solomon in all his glory was not arrayed like one of these. But if God so clothes the grass of the field, which today is alive and tomorrow is thrown into the oven, will he not much more clothe you, O men of little faith? Therefore do not be anxious, saying, "What shall we eat?" What shall we drink?" or "What shall we wear?" For the Gentiles seek all these things; and your heavenly Father knows that you need them all. But seek first his kingdom and his righteousness, and all these things shall be yours as well.

Therefore do not be anxious about tomorrow, for tomorrow will be anxious for itself. Let the day's own trouble be sufficient for the day. (Mt 6:25-34)

In 1 Corinthians 7:32-35, Paul says to the unmarried men that he wishes they did not have to be anxious about providing for a wife and family. Of course he never implies that it is wrong for a married man to be concerned. A responsible husband and father must be concerned but he should not be *overly* concerned. A virtue can become, by excess, a vice.

"For everything there is a season, and a time for every matter under heaven" (Eccl 3:1). This passage can throw light on what

Jesus means when he says: "Do not be anxious about tomorrow, for tomorrow will be anxious for itself. Let the day's own trouble be sufficient for the day" (Mt 6:34). In summer you plan ahead for fall, and rightly so; but if you start planning for the fall in mid-winter, you are going too far. If you start planning today the things you should be planning tomorrow, you are being overly solicitous, overly concerned. As an admonition against this the Lord reminds us of our Father's declared and demonstrated intent to provide for us (Mt 6:30-33).

The second danger is equally clear.

> And he said to them, "Take heed, and beware of all covetousness; for a man's life does not consist in the abundance of his possessions." And he told them a parable, saying, "The land of a rich man brought forth plentifully; and he thought to himself, 'What shall I do, for I have nowhere to store my crops?' And he said, 'I will do this; I will pull down my barns, and build larger ones; and there I will store all my grain and my goods. And I will say to my soul, Soul, you have ample goods laid up for many years; take your ease, eat, drink, be merry.' But God said to him, 'Fool! This night your soul is required of you; and the things you have prepared, whose will they be?' So is he who lays up treasure for himself, and is not rich toward God." (Lk 12:15-21)

The key to understanding the last verse is the first—"beware of all covetousness." Covetousness, the excessive love of possessions, is being condemned, not the laying up of provisions. In God's economy, riches are to be used, not held.

A man "lays up treasure for himself" if he acquires and obtains it simply because he likes possessing it. A man is rich toward God if he acquires and holds it for the right time in order to use it for God's purposes.

"He who contributes, [let him contribute] in liberality" (Rom 12:8). "In liberality" means openhandedly, freely, but also intelligently, not prodigally. A wise man does not give everything away just as soon as it comes into his hands. Being prodigal might seem better than being covetous, because you are not holding on to things, but what is really required is liberality, giving things away when they will do the most good.

As we make provision for the future, we should do so according to three criteria: sufficiency, contentment, and proportion. Applying the criteria of sufficiency helps us to guage whether we are providing too much or too little. What is needed is an amount adequate to the task, but no more. Obviously the person who is responsible for a large family will have to put away more goods than a single person responsible only for himself. What is important is not that one is a larger amount than the other, but that both are sufficient.

Contentment is the wisdom to balance our needs against our desires. St. Paul urges us to be contented with what we need rather than to desire things beyond our need (1 Tm 6:6-8). Often our desires far outstrip our needs, and we find ourselves discontented. Contentment comes from living simply, within our means.

Proportion, the last criteria, is the wisdom to live on a realistic economic level with regard to the times. Because times change, we might need more money simply to eat decently at one time than another. Sometimes we will need more for housing than we do at other times. What we have should be in proportion to the times and in proportion to what we need in order to discharge our responsibilities to the Lord, to our families, and to society.

These three criteria will act as a safeguard against covetousness. The third danger is idolatry.

> No one can serve two masters; for either he will hate the one and love the other, or he will be devoted to the one and despise the other. You cannot serve God and mammon.
>
> (Mt 6:24)

Fear or panic may tempt us to turn away from the one true God, and turn idolatrously to mammon for protection and deliverance. One antidote to this danger is to get our loyalties straight so that fear and panic won't affect us. We must declare ourselves loyal only to God, and renounce any shred of idolatry within us. Another antidote is to make adequate provision, which wards off panic.

Sometimes it is difficult for us to see others getting rich dishonestly and not be tempted to do the same. Dishonesty is the fourth danger we face.

> But as for me, my feet had almost stumbled,
>   my steps had well nigh slipped.
> For I was envious of the arrogant,
>   when I saw the prosperity of the wicked. (Ps 73:2)

The psalmist admits that he came very close to stumbling. If you think you stand firm, take heed. You will be tempted to be dishonest in all sorts of ways. Be on guard.

The fifth warning also cuts close to the bone.

> My brethren, show no partiality as you hold the faith of our Lord Jesus Christ, the Lord of glory. For if a man with gold rings and in fine clothing comes into your assembly, and a poor man in shabby clothing also comes in, and you pay attention to the one who wears the fine clothing and say, "Have a seat here, please," while you say to the poor man, "Stand there," or, "Sit at my feet," have you not made distinctions among yourselves, and become judges with evil thoughts? (Jas 2:1-4)

If times get worse, we may be tempted to show partiality toward the rich among our brothers. Motivated by desire for gain or security, we might think, "If I'm nice to him, he'll take care of me. Why be nice to that other fellow? He can't help me." Scripture warns us against this temptation, precisely because it is one to which we can fall prey.

As I said at the beginning, the one unchanging fact of life is the fact of change itself. We are surrounded by tremendously rapid changes, yet we often act as if the economic future will not change, at least not for the worse. Being provident and resourceful means being realistic about the future and being prepared for what might come. As we prepare ourselves, we must be on the watch for anxiety, covetousness, idolatry, dishonesty, and partiality toward the rich. These are all real dangers for each one of us, but we should not shrink from our responsibilities simply because of the dangers.

SEVEN

Applying the Principles

Economics, money, finances, the possession and distribution of goods—all figure importantly in our lives as Christians. God's point of view on these things, as revealed in scripture and Christian teaching, is found in the principles we have discussed. We have no lasting city here. But while we are here we need to relate to economic systems and structures as part of God's way of providing for all his creatures. We can neither ignore these structures nor retreat from them. His provision for us through these systems has a twofold purpose: to give us sustenance and to give us the wherewithal to support his work. Of the two, his work comes first. It is, then, crucial for God's plan that we be good stewards of our financial resources, prepared for the realities of financial change, and aware of the constant danger that material goods and money present for Christians. However, these dangers should not tempt us to retreat from our responsibility since God has promised us his own strength in dealing with these temptations.

The principles we have considered are intended to form our minds and attitudes, to give us a biblical perspective. Speaking of them as "forming" our minds and giving us "perspective" indicates that they will teach us how to think about money, possessions, and so forth, but not what to think. What we think will be determined to a large extent by the actual situation we face.

Three elements of the current situation were highlighted in the opening chapters of this book. First of all, our life has undergone massive changes in recent years. Part of this change is noticeable in the new set of ideals and values presented to us. We are being told that happiness is a matter of ease and comfort, of doing what we want. The things that free us from other obligations—for example, laborsaving appliances—and which give us the time for ease are not themselves free. Further, those things which make our free time meaningful cost money. Work and money, therefore, have become primarily means to ease and comfort.

Second, and most important, a change has been worked in our character by this desire for ease and comfort. Once self-reliant, strong, provident, and resourceful, our characters have been significantly weakened by a life of ease. Each year finds more of us dependent, weak, improvident, and unresourceful.

For many, happiness rests entirely upon the promises of the economic system. If the system were to fail they would be lost; the meaning of their lives would evaporate. Many are also dependent upon the system for all the necessities of their lives because they despise hard work and lack the skills necessary to approach self-sufficiency. They are weak because they have selected ease and comfort as their ideals.

These ideals have brought with them a kind of selfish individualism. One's concern is only for one's own enjoyment, pleasure, and personal ends. This individualism, coupled with the desire for pleasure, generates a radical selfishness. Commentators have pointed out that the typical American family exhibits the kind of selfish individualism that moves people away from cooperation and a shared life. The average family has a phone, car, television, and a host of other possessions. Often husband and wife will have their own cars and televisions so that each can do what he or she wants, independently.

It is usually considered desirable that children have their own rooms. Most middle-class children don't have to share rooms. As they grow older and conflicts arise over what to watch on television, parents often buy them their own televisions. The same thing happens when they begin to use the phone and when they begin to drive. Each person is equipped with his own things to satisfy his own desires. This type of life-style breeds self-centeredness and makes it virtually impossible for children to learn anything about the give and take of social life, of postponing their desires, or of sharing their lives with other people.

Of all the fields of learning, none gives a better rationale for this individualistic, pleasure-oriented life-style than modern psychology. Modern psychology is the philosophy of our time. It is the most popular subject on university campuses. In the U.S., over 80 percent of college students take at least one psychology course during the course of their studies. A visit to any bookstore will show the great demand for books on psychology. Modern psychology clearly sanctions the hedonistic life-style which has developed in the West over the last century. Some argue that it has not only sanctioned but has also helped to cause it.

A good deal of current psychological literature is taken up with remedies for the problems caused by modern pleasure-oriented society because much of what the psychological theories encourage has come to be itself a great source of psychological problems. Professor Donald T. Campbell of the University of Wisconsin has spoken on the great danger of the psychological approach. In his presidential address to the American Psychological Association, Campbell said that "the religions of all ancient urban civilizations taught that many aspects of human nature . . . for example, lust, wrath . . . need to be curbed" if social life is to work well. "Psychology and psychiatry, on the other hand," he continued, "not only describe man as selfishly motivated, but implicitly or explicitly teach that he ought to be so. They tend to see repression and inhibition of individual impulse as undesirable, and to see all guilt as a . . . neurotic blight created by cruel child-rearing and a needlessly repressive society, recommending that we accept our biological and psychological impulses as good and seek pleasure rather than enchain ourselves with duty."[3] Campbell went on to argue that the ancient way is by far the better, and indeed, the more scientific. The modern way, he maintains, is likely to lead to social and psychological chaos.

What has been wrought in our characters by these changes is the most serious thing we have to face. It is much more serious than either the new ideals of economic life or the weaknesses which we find in the economic system itself. Changes in systems and ideals are one thing; changes in people are quite another.

Third, we must deal with a new kind of economic vulnerability present in the current economic system. The problem is not simply one of escalating prices. The entire monetary exchange and trade system needs to be overhauled if it is to adequately handle the realities of modern economic life. We are operating with a monetary system which has no real foundation; money itself has become a commodity. Trade levels are too high to be sustained by the mechanisms presently available in the world economic system. Geopolitical stresses and strains caused or aggravated by the difficulties inherent in the system threaten us with political and economic instability, if not war.

In our daily lives, this economic vulnerability threatens such necessities of life as housing, energy, food, clothing, medical care, and transportation. These are essentials for contemporary social life and yet the system cannot provide them at a reasonable price, nor in a consistent manner.

Thus we are triply cursed: we have ideal happiness which only the economy can supply; the economy has difficulty in supplying the necessities of life, let alone happiness; the ideal we have accepted has sufficiently weakened us so that we are unable to care for ourselves adequately or to effectively supplement what the economic system can provide. Applying the scriptural principles will provide a way out of this dilemma and offer us a way of responding to our present situation.

The first result of applying these principles should be the recovery of a way of life which is provident and resourceful. We could respond either to the ideal of ease and comfort, or to our own economic vulnerability, or even both together, and still not have addressed the question of personal character. Until we become provident and resourceful people we will be unable to cope effectively with the other realities that confront us.

To do this we will need to get some distance from the economic system of this world in order to gain effective command over the material resources entrusted to us. We are much more thoroughly embedded in the economic system than we should be; too many of our values and attitudes have been twisted to fit into its mold. On the other hand, since God's plans can only be carried out by men of good will making right use of this system, we cannot seek to pull out, but must maintain a prudent involvement in this world system.

One way to get this distance and to gain more control over our economic resources is to cut back or to cut out purchases on revolving charge accounts. The use of these accounts plunges us into the midst of the system, and penalizes us through higher costs. Buying things on a cash basis returns us to a more direct, simple, and ultimately more moral economics. Positive responses might be: getting more involved in your business or work, if by doing so the company could better serve its clients or would be a better place for its employees; learning marketable skills which would allow you to take another job if your present one terminated or if you needed additional income; learning how to maintain and repair your home, appliances, and tools so that you would be less dependent on the repairman and could save money besides. A number of families, a church, or a fellowship located in a city might get involved in collective gardening or purchase a farm. Such a venture would allow them to become more self-sufficient with regard to their food supply and would help them develop useful skills.

The right distance will help us to gain effective command of many of our material resources. We are vulnerable to those who direct the system to the degree that they command our resources. If everything we own has been purchased on borrowed money or on credit, then we are not in command of it; the lender or credit company is in command. This situation can be of great difficulty in times of economic emergency—our cars, our homes, our possessions could be taken from us. Further, not being able to command our own resources can cripple us when it comes to doing the Lord's will or answering his call. A church which depends financially upon the donations of a company which is unjust or uses immoral advertising is not in a position to criticize that injustice or immorality. An individual who has his goods tied up as collateral for loans may be unable to answer a call to the missions.

We also need to look for the signs of the times to come and plan accordingly. If we knew the events of the next twenty years with certainty, we would be in an excellent position to plan, but of course we do not. The position we *are* in calls for a careful analysis of the circumstances possibly awaiting us in the near future, perhaps the next six months, and for a high degree of flexibility in our planning. The economic future is, at best, unstable and dangerous. It might turn out that all these prognostications are wrong—the economy may just limp along without seriously dislocating any of us. Or it could, although this is highly unlikely, get markedly better for a long period of time.

As I worked on this book I had the opportunity to read a lot of futurologists. Futurologists are thoughtful men who study the past and the present and try to make some determination of the future. This is not just guesswork; a lot of weight is given to their thought by large corporations and the military. Among futurologists there is a saying: the future will always be different than you thought it would be. As we consider our responsibilities and try to discover what to do, it would be a mistake to build all our plans around only one specific set of alternatives. We need to be flexible. We should strive to be able to respond well to a number of possible future states. Imagine yourself like a prize fighter, on your toes, able to move in a number of different directions.

A driver on a dark road relies on his headlights to see down the road. He needs to control his speed so that he is able to respond to what the lights illumine, and not "out run" them. The driver cannot see all the way down the road, but he must see far enough ahead to be able to adjust to the next turn. Our economic predictors will not enable us to see very far at all, but we can see far enough to be prepared, perhaps for the next six months. If we stay prepared for the likely events in the upcoming six months, we will be in a position to handle whatever comes our way.

Applying scriptural principles to the elements of modern economic life which concern us has given us four fundamental responses to our current situation. We are to:

1. Develop the character of a provident and resourceful person; train ourselves according to such values and recover such a way of life.

2. Get some distance from the economic system of this world; to be less involved in the system and less dependent upon its rewards and punishments.

3. To gain effective command over the material resources entrusted to us; to use our money wisely, to budget, save, and avoid credit purchases.

4. Develop a flexible plan for the next six months.

What follows will show how to make these responses a reality in our lives.

EIGHT

Testing Your Character

EVERYTHING WE HAVE TALKED about points to the importance
of the development of a provident and resourceful character
or personality for those who wish to negotiate successfully the
uncertain economic times in which we live. But how can a
person judge whether he or she has such a character? Each of us
is provident and resourceful in one way or another. Most of us
have some method of budgeting and could give an account of
where our money goes. We probably are not too strung out on
credit, although we might be strung out a lot further than we
wish. We probably have some kind of savings, or are working on
it. Each of these things—budgeting, credit, and savings—is a
key to provident and resourceful living. However, we need to
assess something deeper, our character.

How would you handle living in tougher times? If you
couldn't have the house or office at seventy degrees all day, if
you couldn't use the car, if you couldn't use the refrigerator, if
you couldn't use your dishwasher, if your stove wasn't working,
how would you fare? Could you find the emotional strength to
keep on an even keel, or would you be jumpy and generally
disagreeable? Do you have enough confidence in your ability to
provide for yourself and others—your children or your
parents—so that you wouldn't be consumed with anxiety and
worry in difficult times?

Many of us have lived or are living in ways that test our
self-reliance and internal strength. As a result, we are becoming
more provident and resourceful people. Many, however, have

not lived this way and are probably somewhat concerned about how we would perform under trying circumstances. For those of us who have these kinds of doubts, a self-sufficiency exercise will prove helpful. These exercises have many benefits: they allow us to test how we would perform under moderately trying circumstances; they test the state of our preparedness for unforeseen economic difficulties; they give us a feel for what the future might hold.

Fundamentally, the self-sufficiency exercise consists of living for a certain period of time (at least two or three days, but a week is better) as if all the external energy supplied to your house— gas, electricity, gasoline—were unavailable. If your household appliances are powered by propane, as they are in many rural areas, they can be used during the exercise since propane is readily stored and does not necessitate continuous supply from the outside. But if you use electricity or natural gas, it will mean not using your kitchen stove, furnace, electric lights, re- frigerator, freezer, etc. Living like this for a weekend or a week can be very instructive.

While the exercise should be a significant test of your situation, it should not impair anyone's health or safety. If it is cold and you have small children or older adults living with you, the heat could be turned down, but not off. If people have special dietary needs which necessitate refrigeration or the cooking of food, then their needs should be taken care of. Water should be readily available—although I would suggest using the outside rather than inside taps—and toilets should be used. The exercise should be carried out thoughtfully, with an eye to the health and safety of those involved.

It is important that the exercise be carried out for a sufficiently long period of time. If the time is too short, the experience could end up more like a party than a real test of how to live under trying circumstances. When I first decided to do this, I talked to two neighbor families and we decided to do the exercise together over a weekend. We pooled our equipment and made a common schedule, sharing meals, recreation, and so on. Two of us had birthdays over that weekend and we decided to celebrate them as part of the exercise. My wife made a cake in a solar oven made out of a potato chip box (it was delicious); we had picnic meals in the back yard (it was summer); and we had bonfires at night with group singing, storytelling, and skits. We had a great time. But we had too much fun. If it had been real, we would not have been partying and picnicking the whole weekend. In fact, life would be pretty grim. Running the exercise with other families is valuable, but it needs to be for a longer time and with a less festive air. The next time, we did it during the work week, which approximated a normal routine more closely than a weekend in summer with two birthdays on it.

The first thing to do is to schedule a time for the self-sufficiency exercise. The next thing is to assess your equipment needs. Since you will not be using the refrigerator or freezer (do not unplug them and ruin your food; just put a piece of masking tape across the door as a reminder not to open it), ask yourself if you have enough nonrefrigerated food on hand to provide meals for the duration of the exercise. This will raise many other questions. How dependent am I on refrigerated foods? Do I have food stored in case something like this happened unexpectedly? Are there ways in which I can keep milk and other foods cool without using electricity?

Next, look at your cooking requirements. During the exercise will you eat only uncooked food? If this were for real would you eat only uncooked food for a long period of time? Since you will not use your household stove, decide what you will use. Many woodburning and kerosene heaters have cooking space on them. Having this kind of stove/heater and enough wood or kerosene would solve both your heating and cooking needs. Campstoves can also be used. I would suggest the propane type rather than those that use liquid fuels (white gas, Coleman fuel, etc.,) since it is dangerous to have those fuels in your home around open flames, and camp stoves that use liquid fuels can flare up. If you use a propane camp stove, I would suggest that you buy the kind of propane tanks found on recreational vehicles and some home barbeques; you can keep the propane outside and run a hose from the tank to the stove as a desirable safety feature. Also, make sure that you have enough fire extinguishers to deal with any accidents.

Lighting is next. Flashlights have only a limited value since batteries do go dead. You will need some kind of lantern or fuel-fired lamp. Camp lanterns will do, but, again, propane is safer. The best are kerosene lamps that use mantles. Aladdin makes an entire line of lamps of this kind; they are highly reliable, produce the equivalent of a sixty-watt light bulb, and are inexpensive to operate. Kerosene is a very safe fuel and can be used and stored inside since it has a very low flash point. Two or three of these lamps will probably be adequate. Kerosene lamps and camp lanterns are hot. They need to be used carefully, and children should only use them when guided by an adult.

If it is winter you will need to be concerned about heat. Are there enough blankets or sleeping bags to keep everyone warm at night? Are there enough sweaters and coats for use during the day? Portable kerosene- or propane-fired heaters are good to use, as is a woodburning stove. Most fireplaces are very inefficient; in most homes they actually take heat out of the house rather than put it in. While you are thinking about your heating needs you should think about the ability of your home to hold the heat. Is the insulation sufficient? Are the windows caulked? Are your storm windows adequate or do they need replacement?

Transportation is an important part of our life. We are used to being able to hop in a car and get across town in a matter of minutes. Our schedules and our work day are often built around the possibility of quick transportation. During this exercise it is useful to reduce the use of your car to a minimum. Bicycling, walking, and public transportation should be used as alternatives.

You also need to consider how washing will be done. Without the hot-water heater or dishwasher how will dishes be done? Do you have buckets or pots large enough to heat water? What about laundry? How will people take care of their personal hygiene? Those who have camped before will have had experience in providing for these needs, but the questions should be asked afresh. Since much of the exercise parallels the kinds of things people do when they camp, it is easy to think that this will be just like camping. Although there are similarities, doing these things on vacation, out in the woods, has the sense of fun and festivity. Living like this in your own home, where you are used to turning on the light, setting the heat, cooking on a kitchen stove, etc., is not nearly as much fun.

Sitting around in a dark, cold house is not much fun, either. What will be the tone of life during the exercise? How do you want to experience it? What will your family do during the free time? It is worth planning some games or entertainment. Music, singing, reading aloud, playing games are all helpful in keeping people's spirits up.

Just preparing for this exercise points out how much we depend on timesaving, low-cost appliances: refrigerators, freezers, stoves, dishwashers, televisions, radios, heaters, furnaces, and so on. Just doing the exercise will probably mean purchasing some equipment and fuel which will force you to reallocate some of the money in your budget.

The following checklist will help you plan the exercise.

—Food: no refrigerated foods; need dried or canned milk, canned food, fresh vegetables and fruits.
—Cooking: no kitchen stove unless it is propane; wood-burning or kerosene heater/stove or camp stoves, preferably propane.
—Lights: no electric lights; need flashlights, Aladdin lamps, or camp lanterns. Again, propane is recommended.
—Safety: fire extinguishers.
—Water: no inside taps; need water containers to store water in the home.
—Heat: no electric or natural gas heaters/furnace; need woodburning stoves, portable kerosene or propane stoves; also need warm bedding and clothing.
—Transportation: use car as little as possible; substitute

bicycling, walking, or public transportation.

—Entertainment: plan games, music, or some other kind of recreation.

—Equipment: ask where you will get this equipment. Will you borrow it? If you purchase it, you need to ask where you will get the money.

—Schedule: figure out time and notify all concerned.

Such an exercise can teach you a lot, both about your state of preparedness and about your character. It can also tell you about the strengths and weaknesses in your family relationships. What you learn can be very helpful in making progress toward provident and resourceful living.

NINE

Credit Purchasing

REDUCING YOUR VULNERABILITY to credit institutions is an important part of getting control of your own economic resources and gaining some distance from certain negative features of the world economic system. In many ways the advent of credit as the normal means of making purchases has been one of the most profound events in the economic history of America. Since it is so important, we need to deal with it in a thorough and practical way. Dealing with the impact of credit on our lives should be one of our highest priorities.

As I mentioned in Chapter One money has changed from a substitute for products in a barter system to a product itself. Credit is nothing more than renting money. Sometimes, in preference to renting a product, we rent money, so we can buy our product. We may end up paying for the money long after we have used up or worn out the product. With a rental agreement we may have recourse should the property prove unsatisfactory, but we have little recourse should the money we rent not buy us what we wanted.

Most of our credit education has come from banks and financial institutions who want us to rent money from them; retailers who are willing to get into the lending business in order to sell their products; and our government, which shows us the way through its own deficit spending. We are always hearing expressions like "Buy now, pay later" or "Take up to twelve, eighteen, thirty-six months to pay." We have begun to accept as a fact that there is no need to wait for what we want. No one advertises with a slogan like "Save now, buy later."

Before buying on credit we should consider some alternatives. Besides doing without the intended purchase, we could consider whether we could borrow the thing we want, whether there are people who could responsibly share ownership with us, or whether we could benefit from renting it. The answers to these questions will depend on what we want or need, why we want or need it, where we live, and who we know. Friends who live in the same neighborhood have countless opportunities for pooling equipment. We might decide to rent or lease something we need, depending on our resources. There are places that specialize in renting almost anything; for one-time usage, we would do well to check on such an alternative.

We might decide to pay cash rather than buy on credit. There is a real cost to buying on credit—whether we pay for it in the resultant markup of the product, or in the finance charges, or both. Many who extend credit raise their prices to pass on to their customers the cost of this privilege. We should find out what the annual percentage rate (APR) will be. This rate of interest paid in the course of one year on the amount of money we borrow. By comparing APRs shown by different lenders or merchants, we may find that we can get our money cheaper elsewhere. Or perhaps we will decide that rather than pay $200 for a $100 item, we could do without it until we can save the $100.

The important point here is to realize and exercise our freedom. We do have a choice and we may choose not to buy on credit.

If I were to develop a range of "probably acceptable" to "probably unacceptable" items to buy on credit, housing would be on the acceptable end. On the other end would be those objects which have no lasting value and which could not be listed as assets. Included in this list would be vacations, groceries, drugstore sundries, and other nondurable goods. It is generally imprudent to buy on credit something we will not possess, like a vacation. It is equally imprudent to buy on credit something we will no longer have when it is paid for, like a bottle of shampoo. There are exceptions, like medical emergencies, for which we must sometimes borrow money. However, you may find that the doctor or hospital will allow you to work out a no-interest payment plan with them directly.

Credit cards are often helpful means of identification, but we should make a rational choice about using them to charge a purchase to our account. If we intend simply to pay for the item when the bill comes in, are we sure we will have the money available at that time? If we intend to pay finance charges, is the item worth the price we will end up paying? If we start adding up the cost, we may just think of a better way to get what we need. If we don't need it, why pay for it? If we are buying on credit because we cannot afford the item, we should consider not buying it at all. If we cannot afford it, and it cannot be borrowed, rented, or substituted for, perhaps we can talk ourselves out of wanting it. Madison Avenue, the mythological source of advertising, entices us to want what it wants to sell. We can say no to advertising enticements and to easy payment plans, and later find ourselves with money for other purposes.

Some see installment credit as a means of enforced savings. "If I borrow the money, I'll have to pay it back, but if I take it out of savings, I won't put it back." If you find it difficult to pay back your savings, get someone to help you. Set up a payroll deduction plan or have someone hold you accountable for it.

Another argument for buying on credit is to bet on increasing inflation. This is sometimes referred to as "paying it back with cheaper dollars." The idea is that if the item you bought today for $1000 sells for $1400 by the time you finish paying for it, and you paid less than $1400 including finance charges, you came out ahead. This argument is based on three assumptions: It plans on continuing inflation; on your continuing to work and/or having money to invest; and on your having increases in pay or investment values. These plans have worked out fine for some people, but not so well for those on a fixed income or those who get laid off.

What about buying a car on credit, or a bedroom suite or appliances? One measure of whether or not to buy something on credit is whether the article being purchased will appreciate or depreciate in value while you pay for it. Houses usually appreciate in value. Cars depreciate, and so do furniture and appliances. Some things have no resale value at all when you are done paying for them; some have long since worn out. A good rule of thumb is not to buy on credit anything that will be unusable when it is paid for. Cars, especially new ones, usually have some value after the loan is paid in full, unless you buy a used car financed by a loan shark. Cars are often a necessity directly related to work, which may mean you must buy one. However, you might look into leasing as an alternative to buying.

The possible savings one could have with leasing is derived from the fact that the leasing company gets a lower price by volume car buying and passes that savings on to its customers. Also, if you are leasing the car for your business, there is a possible tax write-off. The problem is that the leasing company may write into your contract that you must buy the car at the end of your lease, which would probably wipe out any savings you had made. Leasing does not appear to be a sound alternative for an individual under these conditions, but when the new car market is in decline, leasing conditions may be more favorable.

Furniture and appliances can often demand a lot of resourcefulness. One alternative is to rent a furnished apartment while saving for and acquiring furniture. Furniture can be bought used, and refinished or reupholstered. Often, secondhand items can be borrowed or even received as gifts. Some couples prefer to start their families with inexpensive furniture and buy nicer things when the children are grown. In general, borrowing should be at least a second choice. Measure the real cost of buying on credit. Will you have to give up groceries for a color television? Save for it instead of buying now and paying later. Then, if some emergency comes up, you will have money in the bank rather than a half-paid-for color television that you may not even be able to sell.

Some people think that borrowing for an education which will permanently raise their income is a good investment.

However, it is only a good investment if they are sure that their income will increase. In a solid economy, a degree commands a higher income, but many students fail to finish their degree, or fail to train themselves for available employment. Those who have worked, even part-time, before making a decision to obtain more schooling may have a better idea of the job market than those who have concentrated all their attention on school.

What if an emergency does come up? Suppose you have to borrow? Where should you do it? The cheapest loans are usually obtained from family members at no interest. Such loans are notoriously bad for relationships. Problems arise in the absence of written agreements, when both parties have mismatched expectations for repayment and when the loan becomes the focal point of the relationship. The next least expensive way is to borrow from your insurance company against the cash value of your life insurance. (Not all life insurance has cash value.) Should you die, the amount of your loan would be deducted from the payment of your insurance. Credit Unions, if you are eligible, can give the next best rates; then banks or savings banks; then a dealer financed through a bank; then a dealer financed through a finance company; then the finance company; and, last, the loan shark.

Finance companies and loan sharks make their product appealing by making the payment amount so small as to seem attainable. Fifty or a hundred dollars a month doesn't sound so bad until you realize you will pay it for the rest of your life. Finance companies also tend to place a lien on more than the thing you want to buy, often through a second mortgage on your house and/or a chattel mortgage on all your personal property. Defaulting on a loan to a finance company is usually more costly than defaulting to a bank.

Getting into debt is serious business; do not do it without considerable research. An argument can be made for borrowing for a car, and there are times when it is better to borrow than to take from savings. If your savings is a timed deposit and you would pay a $100 penalty or lose all the interest for the quarter by withdrawing it, and if that penalty or interest exceeded the amount of interest you would have to pay for a loan, then it would be better to borrow. Some lending institutions promote borrowing against your savings as being cheaper because the rate is only two percent over the rate paid on your savings. They are not saying it's cheaper to borrow than to take it out of savings; they are only saying they can lend you the money cheaper than the bank across the street. In a sense, they will loan you your savings. With today's inflated interest rates, it may be higher than two percent over their savings rates. If, on the other hand, they are offering you something that will save you money, it is prudent *not* to wipe out your savings.

If you find yourself in debt now, you should begin taking action to get out of debt. Follow these steps:

1. Itemize your debt, to reflect the amounts, finance charges, source, and payment schedule.

2. Discovers ways to save.

3. Consider ways to raise your income.

4. Repay the most expensive debts first, while still paying on the smaller ones. If you have two $1,000 debts, and suddenly you come into $1,000, your future cash position would be helped more by paying off the one with the $100/month payment than the one with the $50/month payment. This assumes, of course, that the interest rate and term of the loans are the same. It would not be true if the loan with the $50 payment only had two payments due, while the load with the $100 payment had eighteen; or if one was at two percent while the other at twenty-two percent.

5. Exercise willpower by not adding more credit purchases.

If the bill collector is pounding on your door, talk to him. Don't be silent. Silence makes collectors nervous, and when they're nervous they sometimes sue. Tell him how you plan to pay off your debt. If you're out of work, say so and tell him what you can do now (even if it's nothing) and what you'll do when you go to work again. Be sure to promise to do only what you can, and then do it, even if it's only five dollars per month. Lenders can be very reasonable if you show that you have good intentions; they may even forego some of their interest if you show signs of paying. A credit bureau or collection agency is likely to be less understanding because it won't be trying to keep you as a customer. Again, the truth is your best defense. Don't be afraid to challenge credit bureaus; they must show you what your record is, and, if it is wrong, they must correct it.

Since we must live with credit, it will pay to live prudently with it. It is normally realistic to buy only what we can afford. The less vulnerable we are to credit institutions the freer we will be to use our money for the things we need.

TEN

Getting Control of Your Money

MANAGING YOUR MONEY could also be called "planned spending." Someone said that money management is a matter of being able to tell your money where you want it to go, rather than wondering where it went. It is an essential ingredient in a provident and resourceful way of life. And although God calls some Christians in a special way to depend on him day by day, many others avoid the tedious task of managing their resources by claiming to trust in God: "God will take care of me," they say. "I don't need to oversee my money." This approach, however, flies in the face of the constant teaching of scripture to exercise responsibility.

Scripture encourages us to be wise, to use our heads, to gain control over the things we are responsible for.

By wisdom a house is built,
    and by understanding it is established;
by knowledge the rooms are filled
    with all precious and pleasant riches.
A wise man is mightier than a strong man,
    and a man of knowledge than he who has strength;
for by wise guidance you can wage your war,
    and in abundance of counselors there is victory.
Wisdom is too high for a fool. (Prv 24:3-7a)

Scripture encourages us to take charge of our money and in such a way that we will be prepared for the future. Not exercising this kind of oversight is a matter of laziness.

> Go to the ant, O sluggard;
>> consider her ways, and be wise.
> Without having any chief,
>> officer or ruler,
> she prepares her food in summer,
>> and gathers her sustenance in harvest.
> How long will you lie there, O sluggard?
>> When will you arise from your sleep?
> A little sleep, a little slumber,
>> a little folding of the hands to rest,
> and poverty will come upon you like a vagabond,
>> and want like an armed man. (Prv 6:6-11)

The world around us tells us, "You earned your money. Now spend it any way you like and you will be happy." Scripture says that we will be content only if we have been faithful stewards.

There is no easy way to be a good steward. It takes work. Record-keeping is a tedious, joyless endeavor. But the good news is that budgeting does work and that you can actually gain control over your resources. When you are in financial trouble and you have not managed your money carefully, there is always the nagging suspicion that something is wrong. As a result you live with a constant anxiety, not knowing where you stand, or when the axe will fall, or the creditor telephone. Without a budget, you are more likely to fall into the trap of spending money for less important items. Vagrants who spend what money they have on alcohol may have no money for food; you might spend your money eating out and not have enough for groceries, where the same money would buy more meals.

Here are some of the reasons for budgeting.

1. It is a tool for making us more provident and resourceful.

2. It will allow us to gain control of our own financial resources.

3. It will help us to decide more carefully where we spend our money and thus free more of our resources for the work of God's kingdom.

4. It leads to more intelligent planning of other parts of our lives.

In approaching budgeting, there are three goals to aim for. The first is to gain control over your income and expenses. This is a result of applying the scriptural principles that we discussed earlier. The second goal is to get out of debt. Finally, you should develop a specific savings program to plan for such things as retirement, the replacement of appliances and other household equipment that cannot be repaired, educational expenses for the children, replacement of cars, and so on. Saving for the future is an essential dimension of the provident life.

Money management means planning, and the place to begin is by reviewing your income. Are you in the right job with the right company? Are you receiving maximum return on your investments, savings, and pension programs? If you need help in answering these questions, don't be afraid to consult some experts: "In an abundance of counselors there is victory" (Prv 24:6).

Review your expenses also. Begin by assembling your check stubs, old bills, receipts, credit statements, and the amounts of personal allowances for members of your family. If you find that you have been erratic in saving these items, resolve to change. It helps to have separate places for storing due bills and receipts of payment. Some people use different envelopes or boxes. I use two different drawers in my desk—bills come in, I store them in one drawer; when I pay them, I put the receipt or a record of payment in another drawer.

As you review your expenses, learn to distinguish between needs and wants. The ability to make this distinction, not only in looking at bills already paid, but at the point of purchase, is essential. Until you can distinguish between what you want and what you really need, you will not be able to get control of your money. This distinction is difficult. Every desire can seem like a need; you must be honest with yourself. Christians can ask the Lord to discipline their desires. The alternative is poverty and disgrace for the man who rejects discipline (Prv 13:18).

Look at each of the major expense items confronting you and ask yourself some hard questions.

1. *Shelter.* Can we afford this house? Are the payments too high? Would we do better to sell it, take our equity, and get a home more suited to our ability to pay?

2. *Food.* Is eating out eating up our budget? How much can be saved with menu planning? How much do we spend on the average, per person, per month, for food?

3. *Clothing.* Do we shop wisely? Are we behind because we buy cheap things that wear out quickly and that turn out to be more expensive in the long run? Do we shop sales? Are we open to buying used clothing?

4. *Education.* Can we afford these high tuition rates? Do the children need to go to nursery school? Is it wise that they are taking music lessons? Can we afford these lessons?

5. *Transportation.* Do we need more than one car? How much would be saved if we sold our best car? How can we cut driving by 20%?

6. *Vacation.* Are there less expensive alternatives? Do we have to leave town to have a vacation? Wouldn't camping be a good alternative this year?

The first step to budgeting is to identify current categories of expense, to examine the amount of each expense, the percentage of your income it represents, and the relative importance of each category of expense. Separate these into three columns.

1. *Necessary, unavoidable items.* This would include expenses for supporting God's work, housing, clothing, food, medical care, education, etc. Be careful what goes into these

categories. Be sure that each item is a *necessary* expense in line with the gifts, responsibilities, resources, and direction the Lord is giving you. If you have talent, music lessons may be a necessary educational expense. Two cars may also be necessary transportation expenses, but perhaps only one car is really necessary. Also check whether the level of expense can be cut back.

2. *Future necessities.* This includes funds for a new appliance, if the old one is giving out, or money to replace the driveway that is breaking up or a car that is on its last legs, and so on. This is basically a category for saving. These items must be ranked, since it may not be possible to set money aside for all of them now.

3. *Nice but not necessary items.* These may be replacements of furniture, rugs, and the like, or added refinements to your life-style, or other items or experiences which can make life pleasant, but which are not essential.

Fill in all the categories under each of the columns until available funds give out. In the rare case where funds are available after the three columns are filled, consider investment opportunities. If you can easily pay all your bills each month, and have a savings account equalling ten percent of your gross annual income, then investment of your surplus funds is a valid consideration.

In a world of galloping inflation, always make a best estimate of an item of expense and add ten percent as a safety factor. Make sure that unforeseen expenses are really unforeseen, and not forgotten; be complete in your survey of upcoming expenses. If you see that you are "running in the red," cut something in order to maintain balance between income and expense. Disaster awaits you if you continue to operate between five and ten percent in the red, in fact, if you continue in the red at all.

Miscellaneous, minor expenses can snowball; these can be difficult to deal with once they get out of hand. It may be necessary to keep a running account of daily expenses for a while in order to get this area under control. Allowances must be adjusted for inflation; not adjusting them can lead to frustration and argument in the family. Follow the government inflation data; it is basically accurate. Credit-buying and borrowing are prime targets for cutbacks: they take money from other categories. Permit no unwise expenditures. Impulse buying can destroy the balance between major expense areas.

On the next page you will find a budget form to be used in getting (and keeping) mastery over your finances. It incorporates our division of expenses into present necessities, future necessities (savings), and nice, but not necessary, items. I have filled in some areas under each heading; you should complete the lists in whatever way is appropriate for your situation. The far-left column records normal budget figures. These are the steps for using this form:

1. Determine your income.

2. Determine whether expenses fall into the category of necessary expenses, savings, or nice, but not necessary, expenses.

3. List all expenses according to their type.

4. Construct a standard budget in column two, recording standard income and expenditures for each item.

5. Compare totals of income and expense. Be sure that income is equal to or greater than expenses. If it is not, either add more income or delete some expenses.

6. When you deposit your check, pay the bills listed on your budget as necessary before writing any other checks. When they have been paid, circle the amount. If you have missed anything, you will know exactly where to look for it the next pay period.

7. Always record each check you write in your check register.

Figure 1: Typical Budget Form

Income/Expense	Standard Budgeted Amount	Pay Periods												
		1	2	3	4	5	6	7	8	9	10	11	12	13
Income														
Total:														
Expenses														
Necessary														
Church Support														
Mortgage														
Life Insurance														
Car Payment														
Future Necessities														
Savings														
Not Necessary														
Music Lessons														
Nursery School														
Total:														
Income-Expense:														

8. If you write a check to cash, make a note of what you intend to spend the cash on, so that you can complete your budget report with that information.

9. Complete your budget report from the information in your check register.

10. Reconcile your bank statement as soon as it comes in; remember banks do make mistakes. If you don't know how to do this, get some help.

11. Work at paying off loans and credit card balances, so that you can be free to use the monthly payments for other categories. (One way to work at this is to stop using the credit card until the balance is paid. Then get into the habit of paying the whole bill when due; if you can't pay the whole bill, consider the alternatives to buying.)

As you budget, you will begin to control where your money is spent, and with whom you spend it. Then you will be freer to spend your money on your real needs, to plan ahead, and to meet your financial commitments. Sound money management is more than good record-keeping; it is a key to living responsibly.

ELEVEN

Goals and Actions

SETTING AND KEEPING to a budget is an essential part of sound money management, but a budget is only a schedule of how you will spend your money during any given pay period. It is not a complete program for managing money. You also need to set realistic goals to indicate in general terms what you want to do with your money. If you don't have goals, there is no reasonable way for you to adjust your budget to new circumstances. Without goals you literally can not know why you decided to spend your money the way you did, nor why you plan to spend it in the way you do.

Any "why" question is a question about goals. *Why* do I spend my money the way I do? *Why* do I save a certain portion of my paycheck? *Why* do I give more to help the poor? *Why* do I continue to buy things on credit? Such questions help us recognize the guiding principles which lie behind the way we handle our resources.

There are four goals which, I think, have to be a part of any worthwhile approach to economic and financial matters. You may add goals to this list, but you should not subtract any.

The first and most basic goal is to use our money to promote the kingdom of God. This goal is essential for any Christian, an automatic part of his economic behavior. Supporting the kingdom means contributing to the Lord's work and giving out of our substance for the relief of the poor. Jesus says that whoever values his life, his possessions, his friends, or even his relatives more than he values the Lord is not worthy of the kingdom. Seek first the kingdom in all circumstances.

Second, we should do what is necessary now to maintain our lives under changing economic circumstances. We know that the economy is none too stable. Even if it were in great shape, the wise person knows that it can change suddenly. As provident people we need to be prepared to provide for the necessities of life when the world cannot, or will not, provide them.

The third goal is to live a full human life. We should move our lives in the direction of quality rather than quantity, simplicity rather than complexity, reality rather than illusion, and sobriety rather than flashiness. Beyond this, we know that life is more than just economic survival. God enriches our lives through sports, music, the arts, hobbies, and the like. We should receive these with a thankful heart and use some of our resources to enjoy these gifts. Some might consider these simply frills that no one who takes the economic situation seriously should engage in. One can indulge oneself, which is wrong, but to refuse these gifts of God is also wrong. A scene from Corrie ten Boom's *The Hiding Place* comes to mind. Even in the worst of times they took care to enjoy the things that the Lord had given them.

> And so our "family" was formed. Others stayed with us a day or a week, but these seven remained, the nucleus of our happy household.
>
> That it could have been happy, at such a time and in such circumstances, was largely a tribute to Betsie. Because our guests' physical lives were so very restricted, evenings under Betsie's direction became the door to the wide world. Sometimes we had concerts, with Leendert on the violin, and Thea, a truly accomplished musician, on the piano. Or Betsie would announce "an evening with Vondel" (the Dutch Shakespeare), with each of us reading a part. One night she talked Eusie into giving Hebrew lessons, another night Meta taught Italian.
>
> The evening's activity had to be kept brief because the city

now had electricity only a short while each night, and candles had to be hoarded for emergencies. When the lamps flickered and dimmed we would wind back down to the dining room where my bicycle was set up on its stand. One of us would climb onto it, the thers taking chairs, and then while the rider pedaled furiously to make the headlight glow bright, someone would pick up the chapter from the night before. We changed cyclist and reader often as legs or voice grew tired, reading our way through histories, novels, plays.[4]

The fourth goal has to do with the conservation of natural resources. God made the resources of the earth to provide for the needs of all mankind. We should be good stewards rather than wasteful consumers.

Goals help us to set specific courses of action. Analyzing the goal and translating it into practical terms will move us toward the accomplishment of that goal. For example, when I ask what it means for me to put my finances at the disposal of the kingdom, it becomes clear that I need to have a regular pattern of support and contributions. I must give a certain portion of my money to my church. If I belong to a prayer group, fellowship, or Christian community, I am obliged to give money to that work also. Scripture enjoins us to care for the sick, the orphan, and the needy, both Christian and non-Christian.

Similarly, in considering the goal of maintaining my life under changing economic circumstances, I must look at the degree to which I am prepared to provide the necessities of life if they were unavailable from outside suppliers.

Food is one essential of life. None of us can depend on an uninterrupted supply of food at the stores. Strikes, blizzards, floods, the high cost of fuel—all might cause an interruption. Inflation continuing to outstrip wages will make food excessively expensive. We need to be in the position of being able to meet our nutritional needs without depending upon outside suppliers. This is, of course, impossible without going full-time into farming and raising livestock, and even then we would depend upon outside suppliers for materials to farm and raise animals. A more reasonable approach is to consider storing food. Any stored food is better than none, but a six-month supply is about right. To try to have more on hand would be a heavy financial burden; having much less would not be protection.

Storing food is a classic example of the provident approach to life. Until recently it was common for people to can food and to put fruits and vegetables in root cellars. Although some people continue to do this, the supermarket and the consumer mentality have influenced many of us to live differently. Storing food is not part of some doomsday mentality. Often we hear of it in connection with some imminent "end-time," but if Jesus were coming soon what would we want food for—to bring a picnic lunch to the Supper of the Lamb? Until he comes, it is a mark of a provident and prudent person to have some "food savings" just as he has financial savings.

Water is another necessity of life. In countries that experience economic hardship, water is rationed. It is turned on only for a couple of hours a day or people must go to a central location and pick it up in containers. If we had a total disaster the government would probably provide some water for our needs. However, pollution of urban water sources, or the inability of rural wells to function because of electrical outages, is a real possibility. It would make sense to have some kind of water filter in the city and either stored water or the ability to generate electricity in rural areas.

Shelter is another necessity of life. A deteriorating economic situation could affect my ability to keep my home. If I lost my job, or had to take a significant cut in salary, foreclosure on my mortgage would become a real possibility. One option would be to try to pay off the mortgage as soon as possible. To do so would use up most of my money, and I would lose a tax deduction in the bargain. A better way would be to save enough money to continue making the payments. If I never needed to do this, I would still have the money to buy groceries and clothing. A good course of action would be to save something like a year's mortgage payments.

Heat, light, and fuel for cooking food are also necessary elements of life. The costs of energy are increasing rapidly. Because of the past availability of fuels and government regulation we have had a false picture of the cost of energy. That is changing as supplies fall off and the government deregulates the prices of fuels. This is, in fact, a strategy used by policy-makers in working toward fuel conservation. As the price increases, we all think twice about energy use. Recently, the National Association of Purchasing Management, which includes those who purchase energy for industry, commissioned a study about the future costs of energy for industrial use.

Middle East countries hold a large portion of the world's low cost oil, and the U.S. will continue to be dependent on them for the next 10 to 20 years. Realizing this, we must be prepared for short-term supply interruptions and price instability. As part of your energy program, it is essential to have contingency programs for any sudden interruption in oil imports. Dual fuel capability, adequate standby storage, and conservation programs should be high on your priority list. . . .

Most price controls on natural gas expire in 1985, so natural gas prices will likely then read parity with fuel oil prices. If, however, Phase II of the incremental pricing provisions under the Natural Gas Policy Act (NGPA) are implemented, then industrial users will taste gas prices approaching fuel oil parity much sooner.

The increase in well-head prices of natural gas permitted by NGPA prior to 1985 appears to average something like 5% to 7% per year in 1980 dollars. This translates into an increase of 15% to 20% a year in current dollars, depending on inflation. However, Phase II incremental pricing could have an immediate and much more devastating effect on industrial gas costs. Ultimately by 1990 industrial natural gas will likely cost over $10.00 per thousand cubic feet in 1990 dollars, compared to the current average price of slightly under $3.00. . . .

The long-term outlook for adequate electric power is not

good. The current conflict between safe energy, a clean environment, and adequate energy supplies has yet to be resolved. If the nation's economy is to continue to grow, we will need energy from all available new sources. . . .

The overall price increase [for electricity] including inflation . . . is expected to range somewhere between 85% and 115%.[5]

The high cost of energy is one thing; its availability is another. Already some power companies are *regularly* shutting off power to their customers. Recently, the *New York Times* reported:

About 12 times a year Florida utilities run out of options and their customers run out of power.

That means, for varying numbers of customers at any given time, their television sets suddenly flicker out and their air-conditioners shut down.

The Federal Department of Energy says that the Florida utilities' practice of "load sharing" or causing selected blackouts of groups of several thousand customers is rare in other parts of the country. The blackouts last 15 minutes to several hours.[6]

If the economic situation worsens we will see more blackouts. It will be a good idea to have an alternate or standby fuel reserve to cover basic needs. Buying new equipment (heaters, lamps, etc.) and large quantities of fuel is expensive. It is also tricky because there are national and local fire codes that govern the storage of fuels. However, if at all possible, it is worth developing the capability to heat and light your house and to cook for a period of six months without the use of externally supplied fuels.

Medical care differs from the other necessities. I cannot possibly provide all the medical care that I or my family might need. I cannot, even working with others, have my own hospital, intensive care ward, and surgical teams. In any real emergency the government would provide major lifesaving medical care, but we should have some first-aid equipment on hand and know how to use it. It would also be wise to have some regularly used medications stored away, on a rotated use basis.

Cash on hand is also necessary for more things than paying the mortgage or buying groceries. We need to "store" cash in a way that would leave it accessible, not tied up in long-term notes. We should store it where it would not have its value eroded by inflation, as it would if it were kept under the mattress. Saving accounts, bank notes, etc., which yield a good return but which can easily be withdrawn without penalty are smart ways to "store" cash.

In scarce times, bedding, clothing, and shoes might be unavailable or too expensive. Make sure that your family is well provided with these items, and that there is sewing and repair equipment available.

Every time I buy gasoline it brings home the importance and expense of transportation in my life. I have already changed my life to adjust to the higher cost of gasoline. Last year we had our family vacation thirty miles from home, not the 500 miles away as we did the previous year. It has made me reflect on the distance between home and work, the fact that we can walk to church and to the store, and that the children can walk to school. I have taken up bicycling. In times of economic uncertainty the cost and availability of gasoline will continue to be a problem. It is wise now to develop alternatives: mopeds, bikes, walking, and public transportation.

Living a responsible life also implies that we need to deal with waste and bad planning in our monetary affairs. Budgeting and careful and wise shopping are all important dimensions of wise money-management. For most of us it will mean changing our attitudes and mentality. For some, this will be a wholesale change, for others, a small adjustment. It does little good to store food against possibly difficult times and continue to purchase useless convenience items. It does little good to begin saving money, only to spend it on things we do not need. Developing provident and resourceful character is the right human approach to money and possessions.

The final goal, conserving natural resources, also has a

number of important action items built into it. Some of them are: conserving energy and fuels, using recyclable and durable goods, and using products and services that do the least amount of damage to the environment.

These four goals will guide us in our financial planning. In analyzing each goal, we have identified a number of actions which, if implemented, would move us toward a more provident and resourceful life-style, and would protect us against possible economic disorders.

TWELVE

Getting Started

EARLIER I LISTED four responses to the present situation formulated on the basis of scriptural principles: to develop the character of a provident and resourceful person; to get some distance from the world economic system; to gain effective control over our economic resources; and to plan for the future. The recommendations give reality to these responses. But you probably find yourself wondering how in the world you can possibly carry out all the things I have suggested. Most of us are playing "catch-up ball"; the initial costs will be great. Either this book will go up on the shelf as another interesting book with interesting ideas, or you will accept the general lines of what I propose and begin to make the necessary changes in your life.

It is challenging, but not impossible and certainly not hopeless. There is a way to get started and to carry through on the actions you decide on. It lies in planning for the future. The overall approach of this book hinges on good planning. You need to draw up your own plan. Reviewing the elements of such a plan will bring it into focus.

Go back to the scriptural principles and think about your life in the light of them. Ask the Lord to enlighten your mind about how they should be applied in your situation. Ask him, in particular, for honesty in reviewing your life.

Next look at the goals set forth in the last chapter. Everything else you do should rest on those goals. As you consider each, ask what you need to do in order to make that goal a reality in your life. The answer will specify the actions you take.

These actions cannot, however, simply be adopted all at once. They must be put in order of priority. In order to determine your priorities you will have to consider the present state of the economy and what it will probably be like in the next six months. Although we are not economic experts we do have responsibility to care for ourselves, for those we are responsible for, and for God's work. Begin with an analysis of the present situation. You don't need a Ph.D. in economics to do this. Just read the newspapers and magazines, pay attention to what is going on in your business, your checkbook, your family budget, etc. I am not recommending a detailed study or precise predictions. I am simply suggesting that you develop some feel for what you think will probably happen, and some reasons why you feel the way you do. Then ask yourself whether, on the basis of what you have learned, it is likely that the situation will continue as it has, or get somewhat better or worse in the next six months.

Now ask yourself about events that would have a significant economic impact upon you and their likelihood of occurring in the next six months. Nuclear war would have a great economic impact: even if you were not dead, it would probably be impossible to get much of what you needed and life would, at any rate, be terrible. But nuclear war, while possible, is probably not very likely right now. On the other hand, in the Great Lakes Region of the U.S. where I live, a blizzard or ice storm could easily knock out the electricity for a time. Within the next six months there is some likelihood of intermittent shortages due to the weather or to truckers' strikes. And of course you never know about the availability of gasoline— shortages come and go, seemingly at random. This six-month look into the future must be continuously updated, and our plans must be correspondingly flexible.

Having listed these likely and not-so-likely events, consider your goals and ask yourself what you would have to do in order to be prepared. When I went through this planning process, I noticed that I depended upon electricity for my water supply (from a well), as well as for lights, heat, and refrigeration. I decided that one of my priorities was to buy a portable home generator. If the high cost of heating your home in the winter is going to affect you, consider a woodburning stove. If food shortages are possibilities, grow your own, or can, or store some food. If these somewhat likely events never happen, the steps you have taken will not have harmed you. In fact, approaching life in this way will have the effect of making you a more provident and resourceful person, and this is important no matter what the economic circumstances are.

The principle we all use in taking out liability insurance is helpful. A given event may have a relatively low likelihood of occurring, but if the impact is sufficiently harmful and the cost of the preventative measure is sufficiently low, the preventative measure may reasonably be taken. If the event takes place, responsible planning will have effectively averted panic-stricken responses.

At this point in the process you should have determined your goals and, with the help of your six-month list of likely events, the actions you will embark upon. The next step is to assign priorities. It would be impossible to do everything at once. The way you order your priorities should be governed by the importance of taking particular actions in the next six months and by the resources you already have on hand. Do not rank them in terms of the amount of money you have to invest: that is a decision that comes later in this process. The order of these items will differ from person to person, but I can give you an example from my own situation. In caring for my family the most important thing for me was to have some food and water on hand for short-run emergencies and shortages. This meant buying a generator and allocating money to buy food for storage. Second, to cover heating, lighting, and cooking, I purchased some kerosene lamps, a kerosene heater, and 150 gallons of kerosene.

After you have set some priorities, compare what is needed with what you already possess or have already done. Chances are that you will not start from scratch. You probably already have some food, extra bedding, and so on. Now inventory your resources against your needs.

Not every action costs money. Put the actions that do not cost

Figure 2: Budget Supplement Form

Action	Month															Cost of Action
	1	2	3	4	5	6	7	8	9	10	11	12	13	14	15	
Monthly Total:																

money on a separate list. Begin immediately to implement them in order of their importance.

Other actions do cost money, and most of us do not have much, if any, extra money. How can we possibly implement these actions on limited funds? It can be done. The key is a decision you have already made to sacrifice some things in order to grow in a provident and resourceful way of life. Look at your savings and see what you have. Next, look to your monthly budget and see what can be taken from it. Where can you cut down to free some money for these actions? Perhaps less money on entertainment or on vacations. Perhaps you could let go of some of your magazine subscriptions. Perhaps you could walk to work, or bike, or take public transportation. Each of us can cut back.

Finally, determine how you will allocate the cash you do have. Make a chart like that shown in Figure 2 (left). This will give you a way of making sure that money is allocated for the highest priority item, and of exercising ongoing control. Consider it a supplement to your monthly budget. In fact, have a line in your budget under necessary items for those actions each month.

Draw your own chart using Figure 2 as a model, listing the actions in descending order of importance in the far-left column. In the far-right column, directly across from each action, list the total cost of that action. Between the left- and right-hand columns list the number of months which you are going to take to accomplish these actions: to be realistic you should probably allow twenty-four to thirty-six months. Now enter the total amount of money that you can spend per month at the bottom of the month column. Ask yourself how much of that fixed amount available to you each month you want to allocate to each action, according to priority.

Figure 3 (next page) provides an imaginary example to show how this works. On the lowest row is the amount of money available through cutting items judged less important. Suppose that the most important action is to save $1,200. This money would be used primarily against the possibility of losing a job, or

Figure 3: Budget Supplement Form with Examples

Action	Month 1	2	3	4	5	6	7	8	9	10	11	12	13	14	15	Cost of Action
Increase Savings	$150	$150	$150		$150		$150		$150		$150		$150	$150	$150	$1200
Emergency Fuel, Lights, and Heat	$50	$50	$50	$150	$150	$150	$25									$625
Improve Clothing and Bedding	$25	$25	$25	$25	$25	$25	$25	$25	$25	$25	$25	$25	$25	$25	$25	$375
Store Six-month Supply of Food		$50		$50		$50		$200	$50	$200	$50	$200	$50	$200	$50	$800
Monthly Total:	$225	$225	$225	$225	$225	$215	$225	$225	$225	$225	$225	$225	$225	$225	$225	

not having enough to pay a mortgage, though it could be used for other emergencies. Second in importance is the acquisition of standby light and heat for the home. Three lamps, a heater, and 250 gallons of kerosene would cost $625. Next, to improve the clothing and bedding situation of the family, it will be necessary to add $125 a month to that part of the regular budget. Storing six months' supply of food will cost $800. These costs are recorded opposite the corresponding action in the right-hand column.

Next, allocate that $225 a month to these actions. Rather than pour all the funds into one action and then into the next, stagger it. This allows progress on a number of actions, thereby increasing the ability to withstand a short-term emergency, which is more likely to happen than a long-term economic disaster. Thus during the first seven months, money for half the goals will have been set aside. The standby fuel, lamps, and heater, the improved clothing and bedding, and the food for storage will have been acquired.

The approach outlined in this chapter will work for you. The entire effort of budgeting, saving, moving away from credit buying, planning, and allocating funds will make decided changes in your attitude, values, and character. In fact, one of the best ways to change your character is to do those things that will force change upon you.

THIRTEEN

Character Formation

MUCH HAS BEEN SAID about actions to meet our current economic system. But all of these actions are valuable only insofar as they help build our character. Many modern business practices or attitudes toward money and goods tend to undermine rather than to strengthen our character. In fact, we do not hear much about character these days. Most of the ways we are taught to think and talk about people come from modern psychology, which concentrates not on character, but on personality. The goal of clinical psychology is to help people behave more normally or learn to cope with their sickness. Most psychological views are attempts to explain how people came to be sick and how they might be cured. It is, therefore, only marginally helpful to the healthy.

Character is different than personality. In Greek the word has to do with the engraving and minting of coins, and conveys the idea of marking or stamping. The English word *characteristic* means those things that mark or identify one thing as distinct from another. Character is what makes a person the individual he or she is. Discussing character is something positive, not negative: it has to do with health, not with sickness. It deals with characteristics of a person and asks what these should be. A person of character possesses positive traits.

Scripture presents us with many examples of men and women of character. The woman of Proverbs 31 is presented as a model. She is wise and she teaches others what she knows

(v. 26); she is loving, kind, and generous (v. 20); she is confident (v. 25b); she is dignified (v. 25); she is strong and takes personal initiative (v. 17); she is trustworthy (v. 11); she is provident (vv. 21-22); she is resourceful (v. 25); she is hardworking (vv. 18-19).

Scripture abounds with men of character, too. Job, Chapter 29, provides us with a picture of the ideal man, parallel to the Proverbs 31 illustration of the woman of God. This passage portrays a man who takes responsibility for the things which God has put under him. He sat at the "gate of the city," with the rulers and governors, because he ruled over those things he was responsible for (v. 7); he was a man of wisdom (vv. 9-11); he was a man of justice and mercy (vv. 12-13); he defended the weak and the poor—"I was a father to the poor, and I searched out the cause of him I did not know. I broke the fangs of the unrighteous, and made him drop his prey from his teeth" (vv. 16-17).

Hebrews, Chapter 11, recounts the faithfulness and courage of Abraham, Isaac, Jacob, Joseph, Moses, and others—men who were faithful despite great personal suffering and, in some cases, torture and death. The men and women that the Bible holds up to us are men and women of character. When we compare ourselves to the great men and women of scripture it is easy to become intimidated. "How could I ever be like them?" But God wants us to be like them and has made it possible.

God made us in his own image: our characters resemble his. Sin has distorted this, but it has not totally nullified it. In sending Jesus, God set about a total restoration of his image in us. He wants us to be marked with his own characteristics, to live his life. He wants us to be able to say with Paul, "The life I live now is not my own; Christ is living in me" (Gal 2:20).

God wants us to be perfect, holy, and blameless before him, like his Son, who mirrors the glory of the Father.

You, therefore, must be perfect, as your heavenly Father is perfect. (Mt 5:48)

For this is the will of God, your sanctification. . . . For God has not called us for uncleanness, but in holiness.

(1 Thes 4:3, 7)

Blessed be the God and Father of our Lord Jesus Christ, who has blessed us in Christ with every spiritual blessing in the heavenly places, even as he chose us in him before the foundation of the world, that we should be holy and blameless before him. (Eph 1:3-4)

Of course, we cannot be perfect and blameless by our own powers. Only God can accomplish this, by living within us. "If a man loves me . . . my Father will love him, and we will come to him and make our home with him" (Jn 14:23). "Do you not know that you are God's temple and that God's Spirit dwells in you? . . . For God's temple is holy, and that temple you are" (1 Cor 3:16-17).

The heroes and heroines of scripture all manifest aspects of God's character. Jesus teaches about those traits, which he forms in those in whom he lives.

Blessed are the poor in spirit, for theirs is the kingdom of heaven.

Blessed are those who mourn, for they shall be comforted.

Blessed are the meek, for they shall inherit the earth.

Blessed are those who hunger and thirst for righteousness, for they shall be satisfied.

Blessed are the merciful, for they shall obtain mercy.

Blessed are the pure in heart, for they shall see God.

Blessed are the peacemakers, for they shall be called sons of God.

Blessed are those who are persecuted for righteousness' sake, for theirs is the kingdom of heaven. (Mt 5:3-10)

These are the characteristics of Jesus himself. He is all those things, and wants us to be like him.

The fruit of the Spirit, described by Paul in Galatians, is also a list of some of the characteristics of God: "love, joy, peace, patience, kindness, goodness, faithfulness, gentleness, self-control" (Gal 5:22-23). The gifts of the Spirit in Isaiah are prophesied about the Messiah, but they apply prophetically to each of us who lives in Christ: "the spirit of wisdom and understanding, the spirit of counsel and might, the spirit of knowledge and the fear of the Lord" (Is 11:2).

Becoming men and women of character, then, involves more than some minor changes in our personalities. It means adopting the very characteristics of God's own life as our own. It means allowing God to restore within us the image of his Son.

How is this done? It happens primarily by surrendering our lives more and more to the Lord, so that he can work his changes within us. This is not a matter of being passive. Character is formed by discipline and training. By repeatedly doing the things that we are supposed to do, by adopting and pursuing the actions set forth in this book, we will begin to develop a provident and resourceful character. However, having the character of a provident and resourceful person is only a part of the larger picture. If we pursue the teaching in this book without asking God to form us in the image of his Son, we have missed the point. Preparing ourselves to meet changing economic conditions is not the most important aspect of the life God has called us to. Nor is developing characteristics of a provident and resourceful person. Loving God with our whole heart, mind, and strength, and our neighbor as ourselves, is.

As we attempt to meet the challenges that the modern world sets before us, we should do it in a way that recognizes the Father's love and care for us: "Some trust in chariots, and some in horses; but we trust in the name of the Lord our God" (Ps 20:7).

Notes

1. Walter J. Levy, "Oil and the Decline of the West," *Foreign Affairs*, 58.5 (Summer 1980), p. 1015.

2. St. Leo the Great, *Sermo 6 de Quadragesima*, 1-2: PL 54:287.

3. Donald T. Campbell, "On the Conflicts between Biological and Social Evolution and between Psychology and Moral Tradition," Presidential address to the American Psychological Association, August 31, 1975.

4. Corrie ten Boom, *The Hiding Place* (Old Tappan, N.J.: Fleming H. Revell, 1971), p. 108.

5. Ralph P. Baker, et al., "Energy-Strategic Long-Range Planning for Corporate Survival," *N.A.P.M. Commodity Committee Reports*, March 10, 1980.

6. *New York Times*, January 4, 1981, p. 13.

Resources

Hundreds of books are available on the topics I have been discussing, some of which are very good. I have listed those books and resources that I know to be both useful and trustworthy.

Self-Sufficiency

1. James Talmudge Stevens, *Making the Best of Basics* (Peton Corp., P.O. Box 11925, Salt Lake City, Utah 84147).
2. Barbara H. Salsbury, *Just in Case—A Manual of Home Preparedness* (Bookcraft, Inc., Salt Lake City, Utah).
3. Howard J. Ruff, *How to Prosper During the Coming Bad Years,* (Times Books).
4. Doris Janzen Longacre, *Living More With Less* (Herald Press).
5. Mike Phillips, *A Survival Guide for Tough Times* (Bethany Press).

Food

1. Doris Janzen Longacre, *More With Less Cookbook* (Herald Press).
2. Yvonne G. Baker, *From God's Natural Storehouse* (David C. Cook).
3. *Deaf Smith Country Cookbook* (Arrowhead Mills).
4. Barbara Densley, *The A B C's of Home Food Dehydration* (Horizon Press).
5. Rosevall, Miller, Flack, *The Classic Wheat for Man Cookbook,* (Woodbridge Press).

Water

1. Lehr, Gass, Petty, DeMarre, *Domestic Water Treatment* (McGraw-Hill Book Co.).

Money

1. Malcolm MacGregor and Stanley C. Baldwin, *Your Money Matters* (Bethany House).
2. Malcolm MacGregor, *Financial Planning Guide for Your Money Matters* (Bethany House).
3. James C. Thompson, *Common Sense about Your Family Dollars* (Victor Books).

Libraries have good collections of books on energy-saving strategies for the home and information on woodburning stoves and the economics of alternative fuels. They also have good selections in the area of skills like carpentry, car repair, and similar topics.

The government prints many helpful booklets which are available at little or no cost. Write Consumer Information Center, Dept. 532 G, Pueblo, Colorado 81009, for a free list.

Periodicals

1. *New Shelter* (33 E. Minor St., Emmaus, Pa. 18049).
2. *Mother Earth News* (P.O. Box 70, Hendersonville, N.C. 28739).
3. *Country Journal* (P.O. Box 2405, Boulder, Colo. 80322).

Suppliers

Martens Health and Survival Products, Inc.
P.O. Box 359
Lafayette, Calif. 94549

Arrowhead Mills
P.O. Box 866
Hereford, Tex. 79045